Just Over the Hill

Just Over the Hill

BLACK APPALACHIANS IN JACKSON COUNTY
WESTERN NORTH CAROLINA

by Victoria A. Casey McDonald

Foreword by Marie T. Cochran

PUBLISHED BY WESTERN CAROLINA UNIVERSITY, HUNTER LIBRARY

DISTRIBUTED BY THE UNIVERSITY OF NORTH CAROLINA PRESS

Suggested citation: McDonald, Victoria A. Casey. *Just Over the Hill: Black Appalachians in Jackson County, Western North Carolina*. Cullowhee, NC: Western Carolina University, Hunter Library, 2012 and 2022.

ISBN 978-1-4696-7203-8 (paperback)
ISBN 978-1-4696-7204-5 (ebook)

Cover illustration: Portrait of Homer Rogers by Victoria A. Casey McDonald

Note: The information contained in this book is not necessarily in chronological order. Every attempt was made to correctly identify each person.

I'M ON MY WAY TO VISIT MY KIN

Just over the hill
Just over the hill
I'm on my way to visit my kin Just
over the hill
Saturday has come
And all my work be done
I'm on my way to my kins' homes
Just over the hill.

—Victoria A. Casey McDonald, 2011

CONTENTS

SECTION I (1825–1900)

SECTION II (1901–1930)

SECTION III (1931–1950)

SECTION IV (1950–1965)

LIST OF ILLUSTRATIONS

Photos in this book are from the author's family collections unless noted below. Photos of less quality (aged/faded) have been inserted because of the significance of the era and human history. This edition is a facsimile of the original publication with a new foreword and image credits. No changes were made to the original text, but a few images have been replaced or updated.

Page 9: "Decks of a Slave Ship," in *The History of Slavery and the Slave Trade, Ancient and Modern: The Forms of Slavery that Prevailed in Ancient Nations, Particularly in Greece and Rome* [Columbus, OH: H. Miller, 1859], Schomburg Center for Research in Black Culture, Manuscripts, Archives and Rare Books Division, https://digitalcollections.nypl.org/items/510d47da-7518-a3d9-e040-e00a18064a99 [accessed August 16, 2021].

Page 26: "The Runaway," in William Monroe Cockrum, *History of the Underground Railroad as It Was Conducted by The Anti-Slavery League* [Oakland City, IN: J. W. Cockrum Printing Company, 1915], Internet Archive Book Images, https://flic.kr/p/oskiQf [accessed August 16, 2021].

Page 28: "Dave Rogers's Farm, 1928," from the Collection of Hunter Library, Western Carolina University.

Page 31: *Music and Dance in Beaufort County*, attributed to John Rose, Beaufort County, South Carolina, ca. 1785, watercolor on laid paper, 1935.301.3, image #T1995-001. High-quality image courtesy of the Colonial Williamsburg Foundation. Gift of Abby Aldrich Rockefeller.

Page 73: Amy Ammons Garza, *George Estus Casey*.

Page 84: Rudolf Eickemeyer, "Wash Day on the Plantation," 1887, Library of Congress Prints and Photographs Division, Washington, DC, https://www.loc.gov/item/97515066 [accessed August 16, 2021].

Page 87: Jack Delano, "Midwife Wrapping Her Kit to Go on a Call in Greene County, Georgia," Library of Congress Prints and Photo-

Just Over the Hill

ACKNOWLEDGEMENTS

Some of these stories developed from newspaper columns from the Asheville Citizens Times, Historic Webster and the Sylva Herald. Others were from news articles in the same three newspapers. Over the years, I had clipped out the articles and columns. Besides these items, I had developed lesson plans on the history of Jackson County when I was a teacher at Log Cabin School. Within those lessons I developed mini-books and task cards for the students to do. Included in this book are three individual stories about African Americans which I used from the packet.

With knowledge of the history of the county and the African Americans who helped make the scattered black communities into one united community, I was able to piece stories together. Therefore I would like to acknowledge Alberta Bryson Stewart, Mrs. Evelyn Austin, Sybil Davis Blakely, Mrs. Ida Allen Bryson, Mrs. Minnie Jo Bryson Jackson, Mrs. Alice Louise Simpson and Stanley Rogers for providing me with details and/or pictures.

As always, I acknowledge my daughter, Tina, who helped me with her knowledge of the computer. Thanks for everything. I love you and adore you.

To all...God Bless.

FOREWORD

*J*ust Over the Hill: Black Appalachians in Jackson County, Western North Carolina* by Victoria A. Casey McDonald could be recounted as part of "the Liars Bench," a casual storytelling tradition among southern men sitting in the public square and at barbershops—folktales of a bygone era for entertainment purposes only. This collection of Appalachian narratives simultaneously steps into the circle of griots throughout the African Diaspora. Although Victoria never lived outside of Jackson County, her appetite for knowledge and her ancestral pride granted her regional and global citizenship simultaneously.

With this reissued edition, *Just Over the Hill* reemerges in the aftermath of an unprecedented year. A decade after its original publication in 2012, the nation continues to face the turmoil of a devastating global pandemic, a sobering racial reckoning, and contentious political conflict. Looking back, the fatal shooting of seventeen-year-old Trayvon Martin in 2012 was an ominous foreshadowing. The handling of that tragic incident in Sanford, Florida, combined with the subsequent acquittal of gunman George Zimmerman, sparked an international debate across all media regarding racial profiling and the criminal justice system in the United States.

I met Victoria in my role as a newly minted visiting faculty member at Western Carolina University (WCU). Our paths crossed as participants in numerous rural activist causes, including the historic campaign for President Barack Obama in 2018. In hardly any time at all, Victoria became my "community ambassador," just as she had for many other new arrivals to the area. These points of reference set the tone for my contemplation about the reissue of *Just Over the Hill*.

The stories here do not possess the lexicon of the Black Lives Matter movement, but they proclaim and confirm the message. The immeasurable value of this book lies in the mysteries between the lines of text and the patterns within its retelling. Instead of a review of *Just Over the Hill*, I am compelled to render a portrait of my dear friend and venerated elder.

Victoria Casey McDonald passed away on Sunday, August 17, 2014. At her homegoing service, a diverse assembly of individu-

1

als from every walk of life shared their stories about a phenomenal woman who was (in no particular hierarchy) a teacher, preacher, singer, artist, community activist, and author. As a Black woman born and raised in the shadow of the mountains of western North Carolina during the era of racial segregation, she moved in a "community within a community." Her lived experience defied category. Affirmatively Victoria was a collector of stories—in the foreword of her first published book, *African Americans of Jackson County: From Slavery to Integration, A Pictorial History*, Victoria recounted the origins of her journey into community history:

> In 1981, Dr. Clifford R. Lovin, a friend and history professor at Western Carolina University, gave me the opportunity to [fulfill] my dream of researching the African American history of Jackson County. "Cliff" told me about the North Carolina Humanities Council mini-grant to individuals that could be presented to the adult population in the area. He gave me the form and I submitted it. Weeks later ... I was awarded funding. Through the sponsorship of the Black Community Development Club of Jackson County, which was under the auspices of Mountain Projects, I was given the task of presenting slide talks based on this research ... which spanned the years from 1865 to 1967.

With the fulfillment of the dream, a grassroots historian was born, and Victoria's contributions made her a regional treasure. Hence, she has been the subject of a wide range of articles and involved in various documentaries and exhibitions including *A Lasting Legacy: Appalachian Women and Their Creative Labor*, organized by the Mountain Heritage Center at WCU. Victoria also conducted oral history interviews for the radio show *Stories of Mountain Folk* on WRGC 540 AM, which has been archived by the WCU Hunter Library Special and Digital Collections.

Invisibility is a theme by default whenever Black Appalachians are discussed. These stories are more accurately unrecognized or suppressed by a "mainstream" reluctant to embrace nuance or the complexity of the American experience. Before the Civil War, Black people made up as much as 15 percent of the population in rural southern Appalachia. Currently, that number has dropped to an average of 3 percent throughout the entire geographic region. The trend of out-migration has been fueled by socioeconomic insecurity. Most recently, the drop in population has accelerated in the midst of the COVID-19 pandemic. In spite of these massive challenges, often isolated and racially segregated communities provide rich, albeit unwritten, stories of resilience and achievement. These stories are integral to the region's identity and enhance the understanding of Appalachia, past and present. I often say, "Small numbers, huge impact."

In 1985, William H. Turner and Edward J. Cabbell coedited the groundbreaking book *Blacks in Appalachia*, which offered the first comprehensive portrayal of the Black experience in Appalachia dating back to the eighteenth century. Notably, Turner and Cabbell were also African American scholars native-born of the region.

In 1991, Kentucky writer Frank X Walker was credited with coining the term Affrilachia alongside a collective that became the Affrilachian Poets, defining the presence of Black people in Appalachia. The term embraces a multicultural influence, a spectrum of people who consider the region home and identify strongly with the trials and triumphs of being in and of the region.

In 2005, two decades after Turner and Cabbell's book, journalist and historian Jeff Biggers released *The United States of Appalachia: How Southern Mountaineers Brought Independence, Culture, and Enlightenment to America*. Among his themes, Biggers stated that academic scholarship rarely captured the significant fact that Appalachia has produced some of the most important American thinkers and creators of African descent, including Carter G. Woodson (founder of the first official celebration of Black history), Booker T. Washington, Bessie Smith, Nina Simone, Bill Withers, Nikki Giovanni, and Henry Louis Gates, to name a few.

It is a challenge to articulate Casey McDonald's impact on the Appalachian region. Undeniably, she distinguished herself through a life of service instead of fanfare, although it is true—even for those who only met Victoria briefly—that her physical presence was unforgettable. She was diminutive in stature at 5'2". Often sporting eclectic colorful clothing, adorned in graying dreadlocks, she possessed a deep contralto singing voice that captivated audiences. Those who knew

Victoria well agree she could be a contrast of personality traits—re-servedly shy in one moment and vocally defiant the next. Sometimes she was the most mischievous person in the room.

Born in 1943 in Peter's Bluff, a Black community of Cullowhee, North Carolina, Victoria was one of ten children of the late Estus and Derosette Casey. In her early years, Victoria worked at the telephone company. Later in life, she earned a bachelor's degree (1973) and a master's degree in education from Western Carolina University (1978) and raised her son Creighton and daughter Faustine (nick-named Tina). Victoria was part of the early cohorts of Black students to graduate from the university.

She began her teaching career at the National Teacher Corps, Log Cabin School, then gave thirty years of service in the Jackson County school system. After retirement, she returned as a substitute teacher, determined not to lose touch with the next generation. Before the term multicultural was a word, Victoria incorporated African American and Native American voices into her classrooms. Yet another aspect of her interaction with youth was her love affair with sports. As a coach, Victoria was a fierce competitor. Her goal was to instill character and self-esteem, not simply put points on a scoreboard.

She was a devoted member of God's Holy Tabernacle of Sylva. As an ordained minister, her distinctive preaching style resonated as a combination of teaching the Word and "sermons in music." She played a vital role as an advocate and organizer, holding memberships and leadership positions in organizations including Bridging Jackson County Communities, Catch the Spirit of Appalachia, the Jackson County Arts Council, and One Dozen Who Care, and she was a char-ter member of the Jackson County chapter of the NAACP.

When AT&T announced its annual call for *The Heritage Calen-dar: Celebrating the North Carolina African-American Experience*, I nominated Victoria for posthumous inclusion. She was selected for the Class of 2017, which represented individuals from a wide vari-ety of fields, including education, architecture, philanthropy, local government, athletics, and media who have made a lasting impact in North Carolina and across the nation. As with previous editions, the North Carolina Department of Public Instruction convened a team of educators to prepare lesson plans based on the lives of the honorees. "Students will see their accomplishments and teachers can put them in the context of history and highlight the diversity which contributes so much to our state's character and heritage," wrote June Atkinson, state superintendent of public instruction.

Casey McDonald's passionate and unwavering commitment to the work of documenting the diversity of Appalachia remains through her quartet of published books documenting her community of western North Carolina. The list includes two novels, *Under the Light of Darkness: Love and Marriage in the Antebellum South for Slaves* (2013) and *Living in the Shadow of Slavery* (2014). She also wrote two history books, *African Americans of Jackson County: From Slavery to Integration, A Pictorial History* (2006) and *Just Over the Hill: Black Appalachians in Jackson County, Western North Carolina* (2012). An African proverb states, "When an elder dies, a library burns to the ground." Yet Casey McDonald's work does not rest in embers. The legacy remains.

This reissue of *Just Over the Hill* was made possible by a Thomas W. Ross Fund Publishing Grant from the University of North Carolina Press to WCU's Hunter Library.

— Marie T. Cochran, 2021

A self-proclaimed "cultural pollinator," Marie T. Cochran was born and raised in Toccoa, Georgia, in the foothills of the Appalachian Mountains. She received degrees from the University of Georgia (BFA) and the School of the Art Institute of Chicago (MFA). She was the 2020-2021/2021-2022 Lehman Brady Visiting Professor at the Center for Documentary Studies at Duke University and the Department of American Studies at the University of North Carolina at Chapel Hill. Cochran is the founding curator of the Affrilachian Artist Project, which marks its tenth anniversary this year. The Affrilachian Artist Project celebrates the intersection of cultures in Appalachia and nurtures a network of individuals and organizations committed to the sustainability of a diverse region. The foreword expands and updates Cochran's tribute to McDonald in the September 24, 2014, guest column of the *Sylva Herald and Ruralite*.

PREFACE

White Americans migrated to the mountains of Western North Carolina when the Treaty of Tellico in 1798 was signed between the Native Americans and the government of United States. That meant that the Cherokees had given up some of their land and white settlers could move into the area. These white settlers were English, Welsh, German and French extraction. However, the largest group was the Scotch-Irish from Northern Ireland, whose ancestry shaped the development of Southern Appalachian society. And it was the Scotch-Irish arriving from the second or third generations of European extraction who brought slavery into the region. It is said that Daniel Bryson came over Balsam Mountain and settled in the Beta area with about 140 slaves. These slaves helped Bryson to clear the land, build his home, and work the fields. He became a prosperous farmer. By 1830, the census recorded two slave owners: David Rogers with eight and John Bryson with one. Because Jackson County had not been officially formed, this makes it difficult to know where its borders laid.

Where did all of Daniel Bryson's slaves go? Perhaps some just escaped back over Balsam or Daniel gave some to his children. At any rate slavery was planted into this mountainous county and remained until they obtained their freedom after the Civil War. When the census was taken prior to the Civil War, there were approximately 277 slaves listed on the slaveholders' schedule for 1860 census. At the age of 78, Daniel Bryson had 18 slaves, D. G. Bryson had eight slaves, and T. D. Bryson had 23 slaves.

Other slave owners were W. H. Thomas, H. Whitmire, and Jno. Wilson, J. Zachery, D. N. Sloan, S. Sherrill, Jno. Mingus, J. Rogers, W. R. Rice, R. M. Norton, J. B. Love, J. McKiney, A. D. McKiney, H. Rogers, P. King, N. Hyatt, E. G. Hyatt, A. Hyatt, W. Hooper, J. M. Hooper, S. H. Hill, J. T. Hackett, Jno. Gibbs, A. Fisher, W. M. Enloe, J. W. Davis, E. E. Davis, W. R. Crawford, N. Coward, M. Coleman, Wm. Cockerham. J. B. Cockerham, A. N. Cockerham, W. H. Brown, Jr., W. Brown, John Brown, Jos. Allen, and N. G Abrams. Just by looking at the names, several of these last names became last names of former slaves who remained in Jackson County and the surrounding counties after the Civil War.

Slavery was deep in the mountain, but not as plentiful as across Balsam. The Cherokees owned slaves, also. They looked at what the white society did and copied them. History tells us that the Cherokees, being influenced by the white Appalachian culture, strived to also create a civilized culture of like nature. The Cherokees believed that by owning slaves, that made them civilized. And yet their slavery was different from the white society. They insisted their slaves were their brothers.

With the 1860 slave schedule, the slaves in Jackson County appeared to be in a family unit with a male or female slave head of the household. Slaves were chattel property, but they were more than that. They became members of the slave owner's family. Therefore when the Civil War broke out, the slave owners left their trusted slaves in charge of their homes. These slaves were to defend the home and take care of the womenfolk and children.

Hence, this book is divided into four parts. The first section is stories of loyal slaves who served their master during the Civil War and how they fared after the Civil War. The next section is stories from 1901 until 1930 as the former slaves created their own society with the realm of the white Appalachian society. The third section tells stories of how the scattered African Americans communities developed into one. The fourth section 1931-1965 relates the decline of the united African American community.

Within this book are the stories of different individuals, jobs, incidents, etc. and how these individuals and incidents impacted the African American community, as well as Jackson County society as a whole. Some are even love stories. From slavery until to tomorrow, we African Americans have contributed to the greater development of Jackson County. We had leadership in our community, which held us together. Granted the details of some of the stories have been embellished, but the central thought is there. May you enjoy and be blessed by these stories.

— Victoria A. Casey McDonald

Just Over the Hill
SECTION I
(1825-1900)

INTRODUCTION

The history of the African Americans in Western North Carolina began long before the Civil War. As mentioned in the foreward, in the early 1800's, Daniel Bryson herded 140 slaves into the area that was to become Jackson County from across Balsam Mountain and settled in the Beta area. Others came across Soco Gap. Slavery became a way of life for about a third of the white population. Most of these slave owners had less than ten slaves. Therefore, most masters and his slaves worked together in fields.

With this working relationship between the slave and master, there was a close bond. In the census on the slave schedule of 1860, it appeared that most slaves lived within a family unit. Sometimes, the master had to sell a slave for debt or give a slave as wedding gift to their daughter.

When the Civil War began and the master went off to fight for state's rights, while trusted slaves were left behind to take care of the master's home place. Other slaves went with their masters as a body servant. In the individual stories told through the eyes of the slaves or former slaves, one can see that the African Americans defended what they believed was their homeland.

As you read these stories of the African Americans in Jackson County, one can see the trust the slave owner and slave had between them. In other words, the slaves found a safe haven in these mountains when the Civil War ended. To survive, the former slaves relied on the whites to nurture them until they realized they needed to establish their own churches, schools, social organizations and their own businesses or professions.

The slaves who "jumped the broom" had their marriages legalized. Thus the African Americans began to create their own communities, which were situated just over the hill from each other. Most African Americans lived in a community that had a white Appalachian living next door.

Where It All Began: My Great-Great Grandmother

*(From the West Coast of Africa, to a Caribbean Island, to
Virginia, to the mountains of North Carolina)*

Oconaluftee

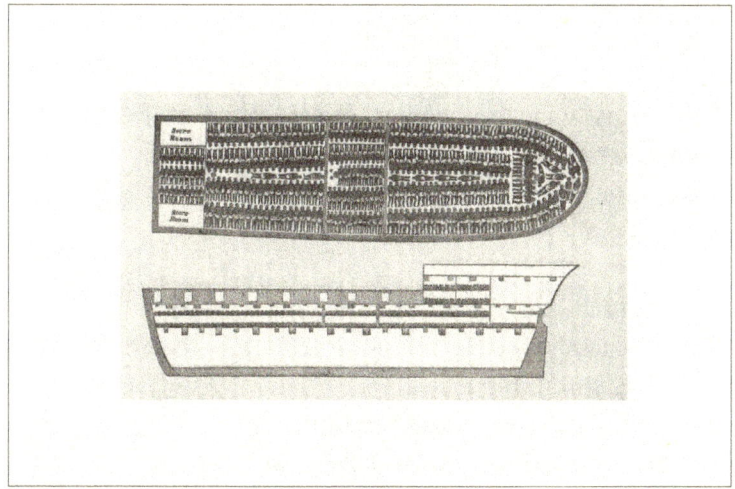

Stripped from our homeland
Held in a dungeon down by the riverside
Waiting for our fate
Looking at some strange being with hair on his face
An animal, not from the rainforest, to eat our dark meat
Who were these strangers?
What did they want from us?
What was our crime to be chained like an animal?
Questions that had no answer!
We were Africans, but we were the strangers.

We looked at each other with fear in our eyes
What would be our fate?
Words we could not understand shouted through the gloom
Cat-of-nine-tails whipping our backs
In chains we moved and followed them.
The sandy shores of my homeland squeezed between my toes
Leaving a perfect footprint for someone to follow,

But when I looked back, it was gone
Mangling in the sand with other footprints
And I cried because I knew it was gone.

The ocean waves were angry now,
As we are piled into a small boat, chained together
Looking way out beyond the waves
"What is this I see?
Water, water, water, surrounding us
Like the solid earth would never again exist!"
I shouted my ancestors' names, but it fell on deaf ears.
A bigger, stranger boat bounced on the horizon
"Will this be my home?
Will this be my home?"

We are herded on the boat like the wilder beast
Whipped and shoved, trying not to entangle the chain
Some of us stumbling down
But the whip demanded us to get up.
The breeze from the ocean was now on our faces
The smell of salty water filled the air.
We breathe in deeply, as they herded us down below.
Into a dark, dark hole with little fresh air
I smelled the remnants of human remains
And I know I will be forever lost!

Chained in this dark, dark hole
Together with people I did not know
What was my crime?
The splashing water against the boat sang a song.
It said, "Gone are the days when my heart was happy and gay.
And yet my ancestors will know me not
I am nothing. .. A piece of black meat!
Lying here, waiting to be devoured by pale hairy creatures.
Let me die! Let me die!"
But somehow I willed my soul and body to live.

Days turned into nights as nights turned into days.
Eat, sleep, relieve thyself, and breathe in the stench.

How long I did not know. . .
But fresh air came through the dark, dark hole.
Land was near and I was still alive.
"Where are we?" my soul cries
The hatch was opened one more time
And the chains loosed from my bed of horror
A few of us were herded on deck
To be free! No...just to be cleaned up.

The stench of the bowels still in my nose,
As fresh air strangled my very soul
Water still seemed to surround us
An inner being shouted, "No, no, no!"
For this was not my homeland
Only strangers I'm to see
Voices I could not understand, speaking all around me.
"Who am I?
I am an African.
I am lost in a world I do not know."

We have landed on some island
About the size of my kingdom abroad
But no land seemed to be near us
Even the Natives seemed to stand in "AH!"
Of the bearded strangers who have taken control.
I was to begin my life all over again
Reborn into their way of life
Everything taken away from me
I was a person without a country
I was a person without a name.

I was drilled into submission
I was a helpless, flightless bird
My wings have been broken
I have learned to know my new name
My African birth name now forgotten
I have been seasoned
My life started anew in this strange world
I heard words like "...the mainland...."

"Where can that be?"
I was sold at auction.

"Martha. . . Is this really me?"
Sold to a slave captain to be taken to the mainland
The mainland in a place called Virginia.
Put back in the bowels of a ship
Back to stench and horror,
But I listened and I had learned
I know now that I was a slave
And yet I wondered how long I would be enslaved
Not until death, "Just do as you're told!
Freedom will come!!!"

Virginia. . . The port was very busy,
Buzzing with people, mostly with white people
Dressed in what I knew was their Sunday best
Walking with canes to try to look important
Examining us...slaves...like we were cattle
To be bred on the plains of Africa
I tried to think of my homeland
For a slave was important to the kingdom
People were an asset, not property...
"Am I just a piece of property!!!"

Standing on the auction block, shivering in the heat of the day
I looked at all the buyers and tried to find a kind face.
Bearded ones, I could not see, their faces were hid
There was one who face was clean shaven
His piercing eyes seem to crawl out of their sockets,
While no smile crossed his white face
I looked away from him, as he looked my way
Was there kindness there?
"Who am I to say?
Who am I to say?"

The auctioneer did his thing to sell us
He made us hold our head erect.
He made us show our teeth

He felt our arms to tell them that we were strong
Good to work in the field
Strong!
Strong enough to endure the pain of lost identity
Strong enough to endure the stench of human waste
Strong enough to begin a new life
Strong enough!!

I was bought by William Holland Thomas
Taken away from Virginia to a place called North Carolina
In the hills of North Carolina, I went
And there I was indoctrinated into the culture of the day.
Yet would I stay there?
Would I be sold again and again?
Never knowing if I belonged.
Submersing myself into a new, unfamiliar, culture
This Appalachian culture
That my descendants now call . . .
                                    their ancestral home.

Amanda Thomas: My Great-Grandmother

Stekoa Fields, Montieth Gap

Amanda Thomas was born in Stekoa Fields which was the name of William Holland Thomas's home. According to her death certificate, she was born on July 3, 1839. My great-grandmother was a slave of Thomas and her mother, Martha, was the first slave he purchased. Traditionally, it is stated that in 1825 Will Thomas went to Richmond, Virginia and purchased her at an auction. At the time, Martha was about eight years old.

Very little is known about Martha or Amanda, but it is known that Amanda smoked a corn cob pipe. Growing up around Stekoa Fields, she knew the Cherokees. When she was fifteen, Will Thomas married Sarah Love from White Sulphur Springs near Waynesville. It was perhaps through this marriage that Amanda met her husband-to-be, William (Bill) Hudson Casey. It seemed that William's older brothers, James and George, were conscripted for ninety-nine years to James R. Love, Sarah's father.

With the approaching Civil War, it is traditionally stated that Mr. Love was gathering strong young bucks to defend his home. It appears that Bill's mother Harriet was a free black person, but conscripted her sons to Mr. Love. Bill was too young to be conscripted.

At any rate, Amanda and Bill probably cohabited as the Civil War was raging, or shortly after the war. Like most slave marriages, they could have jumped the broom. Three years after the Civil War, Amanda and Bill legalized their marriage. On January 14, 1869 they were married by the Justice of the Peace, C. C. Spake.

In 1866 Amanda had a child. On his death certificate, Bill Casey is listed as his father. They named him Mountville Sherman. Researching the Civil War history, Mountville was a name of a small town in Virginia. In 1861, the North and South fought a battle there. Perhaps, she heard about the battle and named her first born son Mountville.

His middle name Sherman was a common name that many former slaves named their male child. Just listening to the feats of General William T. Sherman march through Georgia destroying the Confederacy, Amanda believed that she would be free. By destroying town after town meant that slavery was ending.

The war ended just shortly before Mountville was born. Although Bill and Amanda were free, they continued to live at Stekoa Fields. As matter of fact, all her six children were born there.

In 1892 in the Township of Webster, Bill and Amanda purchased land. At that time Webster's boundary went all the way to Cullowhee, which included Montieth Gap. They bought a mountain tract from M. L. Deitz and his wife D. J. Deitz for $300 dollars. The deed stated…"To have and to hold all the appurtenances there…to belonging including wood, water, minerals, fossils, etc. To have and hold onto the use of the said William Casey and his heirs and assigns forever." At the time of the purchase, Mountville was twenty-six and baby Charles was eight. While the children felt that they were living in slavery, the purchase of the land made them feel free. Bill must have felt really free, because he left Amanda and went to live with Rosette Hyatt in Little Savannah.

With Bill gone, Amanda became the matriarch of the Casey family. Along with her oldest son, Mountville, she held the family together. When Mountie died in 1914 of typhoid feverher second oldest son, George Power, took over. In 1905, he had married Sadie Hooper. Within Amanda's household was her extended family, which included her daughter Cordelia and her two children, Robert Lee and Cary May.

Amanda saw many changes. Along with George's wife, she wanted her grandchildren to have an education. From the one room school to a consolidated one in Sylva, she praised God for it. On December 8, 1924, Amanda died at 4:30 am from pneumonia.

Long Journey Home: Granny Ede

East Fork Community

In about 1825, slavers in Guinea on the west coast of Africa took a little African five-year-old girl with blue eyes and her mother. With other Africans, she and her mother found herself on the sandy coast in chains. There were Africans of different tribes with languages she could not understand. Chained with her mother, they did not know what fate awaited them.

The bearded-faced slavers spoke a strange language, but their action told the little girl and her mother that they wanted them to get in the small craft to board the big boat lying off the coast. Without knowing where they were going, the two were forced on board by foreign men who ordered them into the craft. Her mother protected her as the other Africans crowded in on them. Frightened they huddled together.

When they got to the slave ship, the crew chained them together in the hull of the ship with the others. There was no space to sat up, so they laid side-by-side all though the journey to a new land. The ship rocked and rolled. Roaring water slapping against the hull of the ship was like a continuous rhythm that frightened them. Moans and groans filled the stagnant air, while the smell of feces and urine made the children sick. Others died and the bearded white men dragged them out. From time to time, the crew herded them up on the deck and cleaned the hull.

At last, the ship docked in Virginia. The motion of the waves stopped. The hull hatch opened to a blue sky, which welcomed them. The fresh air forced itself in their nostrils and the little girl wondered if this was the end of her journey. Her father had remained in Africa and she was somewhere across the big water. Her only family was her mother, who tried to protect her.

The next day, all the Africans were put on the "Slave Block." Mother and daughter held on to each other. It seemed they did not want to be separated. They did not know the strange language, but it appeared that the other Africans were being sold. She saw money exchange between the white men after the bidding was over.

Now they stepped up on the block. Men came and examined them. They looked at their teeth as if they were horses. They felt their arms and legs to make sure that their limbs were strong. The girl hugged her mother as the white men bidded. A family living near Petersburg bought them. The first thing that the family did was to take away their African names. The little girl's name was changed to Ede and her mother became Chloe. Slowly they learned English and worked for their Master and Mistress.

However things didn't work out, the mother was sold on the Petersburg slave market. Now eight-year-old Ede was all alone and working in the tobacco field. She could crush a tobacco beetle with her bare hands and handle the hoe like an old pro.

Shortly after that, Joshua Hall of Maryland bought her and two boy slaves, Sid and Icem, who had no immediate family. Ede considered them her family. They were younger than Ede and she protected them.

Joshua came to the mountains of North Carolina to live. His parents, Mr. and Mrs. John Hall, came to Burke County, but Joshua continued westward with his three slaves. He settled in Webster and met Jane Queen. They fell in love and married in 1829. Joshua settled down and raised a large family. He was a gentleman farmer and a Baptist minister and kept Ede, Icem and Sid together. Together the slaves and the Halls worked the land.

It seemed that David Fonsey Hall, Joshua and Jane's oldest son now owned Ede and her two siblings. Around the 1840's, Major Higdon, sheriff of Macon County (Jackson County had not been formed) owned a farm in the East Fork Community. High Sheriff Higdon allowed himself to get in debt, forcing him to sell the place at a public auction. Dr. John Woodfin bought the property. David saw this piece of land as an opportunity. The farmhouse was two-story structure, which had slave quarters connected to the back of the house. It was ideal for David and his growing family. Short on cash, David exchanged Sid and Icem for the farm.

Ede was hurt. She could not understand why David sold Icem and Sid. They were family. Icem and Sid served Joshua and Jane faithfully, now David just up and sold them for a piece of land (Riverside). It was not like that; they married and moved away, they were sold. Through it all Ede protected them. Now, she could not. For the first time, she realized that she was just chattel property. She had helped raise David, but she had no say in who was sold.

It would be far and between before she saw her foster siblings again. She was pleasant to David Hall, but she did not like him. However, she loved his wife and children. Now, they were the only family she knew. Affectionately they called her Granny Ede. She was a second mother to the Hall children.

Before the Civil War, David Hall freed most of his slaves. Ede got her freedom papers, but she occasionally stayed at Riverside. At the back of the house was her room and the family welcomed her. During the War, when David marched off to "whup the Yankees," Granny Ede stayed at Riverside to help.

Although Granny Ede spent a lot of time at Riverside, she married Robert Love and had one daughter Anne. She ever learned to read and write. In her humble life, she graciously served four generations of Halls. On January 17, 1917 at the age of 100, Granny Ede died. Some say she still haunts the rooms of Riverside. Alan Thornburg stated, * "...on more than one occasion, I've seen what I believed to be the image of an old black mammy swaying quietly in a large rocker." And you can bet she was smoking her clay pipe.

*Historic Webster

Cudge Thomas: Just a Body Servant to My Colonel
Whittier/Dillsboro

When North Carolina seceded from the Union and joined the Confederate States of America, Senator William Holland Thomas suggested that a battalion of Native Americans from the Qualla Boundary be formed for the local defense of the Carolinas, Virginia, and East Tennessee. Thomas was the white chief of the Cherokees who had saved the Qualla Cherokees from heading to Oklahoma on the Trail of Tears. Major Washington Morgan formed the group of Native Americans on April 9, 1862 and the Native Indians chose Thomas as their captain, who later became Colonel Thomas. There were about 130 men, including a dozen white mountaineers in this defense group.

Although Thomas was a champion to the plight of the Native Americans, he held Blacks as slaves. Among them also was Colonel Thomas' body servant, Cudge, a fifteen-year-old slave who was born June 9, 1846 to an unknown mother and one of Thomas' male slaves, Jim. Cudge and his father were two of the 38 slaves held by Thomas. It seemed that Cudge's father was a trusted slave, who often traveled around Jackson County carrying messages and deliveries for his master.

He moved about freely as he attended to Thomas' affairs. Not only was he a trusted messenger, but he was allowed to have his own account at Thomas' store. He utilized this privilege by purchasing his own clothing, food and tobacco. At least on one occasion, he went to Tennessee to deliver $350.20 for Thomas and he took his son with him.

Now, too old to travel, Thomas took his son Cudge as a body servant to accompany him in Raleigh when he attended the General Assembly. Therefore, it was apparent that Cudge Thomas would join the Confederate Army and serve his master when the war broke out. Traveling was not new to Cudge as he helped his master prepare to defend East Tennessee from the Union invasion of the Confederate States of America. To the slave, it would be another adventure to tell his children and grandchildren.

***

It is now September 18, 1915. In Dillsboro, the sixty-nine-year old Cudge Thomas is sitting on the front porch of his home, as Jackson County's old Confederate veterans gathered on Courthouse Hill for the unveiling and dedication of the Rebel soldier monument. Reflecting back, Cudge remembered his experience in the Civil War.

"Being Colonel Thomas's body servant, I went everywhere with him from the mountains of North Carolina to capital of the Confederate States. When we started, Colonel Thomas led the men from Qualla to Webster, then on into Macon County. Most of the men were Cherokees. I grew up with a lot of them. I watched as other Cherokees joined the company.

"In two days, it seemed like we marched a hundred miles to this little town called Valleytown. My job was to take care of Colonel Thomas' horse, polish his shoes, shave him, and put his clothes out and other personal things. I had promised Miss Sallie that I would look after him.

"I remember that it rained like cats and dogs. I went to Colonel's side with a rain slicker to put over his shoulders. Within a few hours, the rain caused the river to rise making it impossible for us to get across. All night, we had to camp there. The next morning we marched out of there and made it to the Tennessee line by nighttime. There we set up camp again and marched after a quick breakfast the next morning and by noon, we had arrived at Sweetwater, Tennessee."

Cudge smiled, "To me, this was familiar territory. I had traveled this way before. As I held the reins of Colonel Thomas' horse, I listened to him talking to another officer. It seemed they were going to ride the train to Knoxville.

"Colonel Thomas told me to take their horses to the railroad station and put both horses in a boxcar. I rode in the boxcar and took care of the horses."

"Why, Grandpa?"

"Serving Colonel Thomas was my job. I never joined the Confederacy as many Southern blacks did. However, from 1862 to 1865, I watched over Colonel Thomas. I saw his political mind at work when he talked to the Unionists who lived in the towns and countryside that Thomas' Legion defended. In what they called the Valley Campaign, we were almost wiped out. Men were falling everywhere.

"After the fighting at Cedar Creek, Colonel said that less than 50 or so men reported for duty. We lost a lot. Some died, while others just ran away."

"Why, Grandpa?"

"They were frightened. Some of them returned and the Colonel accepted them. The higher up didn't like that. No siree, it seemed that deserters needed to be shot."

"Why, Grandpa."

"You don't run away from fighting. You gotta stand and fight."

Cudge shook his head sadly, "They caused my Colonel to be courtmartialed. To me, he was just trying to do his job. You need men to fight a war, don't you?"

"Yes sir."

"I just didn't understand. They arrested Colonel Thomas sometimes in the fall before the war ended and sent him down east to Goldsboro for trial. I went with him. They said that my Colonel was entertaining deserters. That was conduct unbecoming an officer and a gentleman. Said that he couldn't discipline his troops. All lies. Colonel knew what he was doing. He knowed how to run his business. They found my Colonel guilty, but he didn't give up. No siree, he fought that sentence.

"That's when we went to Richmond to see President Davis. I saw President Davis. He was nothing like the picture of Abe Lincoln. Just like Colonel Thomas, he didn't have a beard. Clean shaven face. I just knowed that he had a body servant who took care of him."

Cudge scratched his balding head. "Strange, real strange!"

"What, Grandpa?"

"Well, President Davis had a colored boy who sat at the dinner table with the family."

"Did you eat at the dinner table?"

"No, child! I was just a servant. I ate in the kitchen with the rest of the house servants. Don't know the relationship between President Davis and that colored boy and I didn't ask."

Cudge cleared his throat and continued with his tale.

"You know, President Davis listened to the Colonel and he overturned the guilty verdict. Finally, we went back to his men. When they didn't have what they needed, Colonel Thomas used his own money.

"After the war, I was freed and came up here to Dillsboro. I married your grandma Mary on October 22, 1874. She was one of them pretty Bryson gals. She got me to going to church." He laughed,

"I became a member of River View Baptist Church. Best thing I could have done. It helps when the nightmares of the war creeps into my head."

Sadly, Cudge shook his head. "But poor Colonel, his health failed him and he spent most of his money for the cause for his Cherokee people. He's dead now. I heard that he died about twenty years ago. The war really got to him. He kind of went crazy. They sent him to the Crazy House."

"What about you, Grandpa? Why ain't you in Sylva celebrating with the other war veterans?'

"I was just a body servant to my Colonel."

Someone reminded the government that Cudge Thomas had served the South's cause to protect their states' rights. Therefore, in 1934, at the ripe old age of about eighty-eight, Cudge Thomas who served his master well doing the Civil War received a semi-yearly pension as a Confederate Civil War veteran. However, the next year, Cudge died on March 12, 1935. He is buried in the Parris Cemetery among the un-  known graves. Although, there are no grave markings, the evidence is recorded in the Register of Deeds office in volume # 22 on page 40 in the County's Death book.

Pinckney Crawford: The Balsam Defender
Balsam

When the Civil War came across Balsam Mountain, there were folks to defend the insurgents. Reverend William R. Crawford who lived in the Addie Community had five sons go off to war to save the South. Preacher Bill as Rev. Crawford was known around Jackson County was busy taking care of other folks spiritual needs, so when he left the farm, his wife, his young daughters and four sons handled it. He also instructed three slaves to help run and to defend the place from Yankees.

According to the 1860 Slaveholders schedule, there were two female slaves and one male slave, all living in the one slave cabin on the place. Judging by the ages of the slaves, it appeared that it was a mother and her two children. The older female slave was Black and 30 years old. The two younger slaves were listed as Mulattoes, which meant that they were half-black and half-white. The female was eighteen years old and the male was twelve years old—Sarah, Elizabeth, and Pink

A. J. (Andrew Jackson) Crawford, the preacher's son wrote to both his mother and father in separate letters. In his letter to his mother, he asked her to tell the family to write him. He identified each male member with his initials and last name. At the end of the sentence, he asked Sarah, Elizabeth, and Pink to write him.

It is not known whether Preacher Bill brought the three slaves with him when he came to mountains of North Carolina in 1850 when he purchased 50 acres of land for $50 dollars.

Settling down in the Balsam community, he and other members of Scotts Creek Baptist formed their own church in June 1852, which they called Mount Pleasant Baptist Church. In Mount Pleasant church registry, Sallie a Black woman was listed as a member, whom most believe was Sarah, Preacher Bill's slave. It is not known whether Pinckney and Elizabeth joined Mount Pleasant. Even the relationship between the three slaves is questionable.

At any rate at the time of the conflict, the young boy would have been about thirteen or fourteen. Being the only family that Pinckney knew, he was a trusted, loyal slave. Like most slaves in the mountainous region, they were treated like a member of the family. When work in the field needed to be done, slave and master labored side by side. It was natural that the slave would protect their master's land.

The war raged for five years. During that time, the Unionists and Confederates fought each in this mountainous area. Some Confederate soldiers turned on their Southern homeland and fought with Unionists. It became the battleground for Unionists and Confederates in an irregular war that touched every citizen in the region. These bands of men were not regular soldiers, but men looking to raid and loot the countryside.

Pinckney took his master's word to heart. There was not going be any Yankees robbing and stealing from the Crawford homestead. He was going to run them off any way he could. It is related that Pinckney, (G.W.) George Washington, and Mariah, Preacher Bill's youngest children defended their home from raiders, whether they be Rebels or Yankees.

As the war devastated the countryside and both armies could not provide food and clothing for their men, they began to rob and loot the mountain folks. Deserters, sometimes a combination of both Yankees and Rebels, roamed the mountain in search of farms where the men were away and they could easily take food and clothing.

One time, when they came across Balsam and approached the Crawford homestead, they encountered an army of children led by Pinckney.

This army was not armed with guns and bayonets. They had pitchfork, axe, hoe, or sticks to drive away the raiders. Not only did they chase them away, Pinckney shouted at them.

"Go out of here, you damn Yankees!"

The Crawford children joined in the yelling and this brought out Mrs. Crawford with a rifle in her hands. It was cocked and aimed at the leader of the raiders. With all the commotion, the raiders moved on. The Crawford homestead was safe once more. Those insurgents who roamed the mountain most likely heard about the Crawford homestead and stayed away. Pinckney had saved the day. How many times did he defend his home? It is lost in history.

However, Pinckney remained at the Crawford's after the Civil War. Months at a time, he left, but he always came back home. Preacher Bill and his offspring welcomed him. The room in the back was always waiting for him. When he died the Crawford family buried him in the family plot.

Unlike Cudge Thomas, Pinckney did not receive a pension for his defend of his master's home. However, Pinckney's gravesite is marked in the Crawford Cemetery.

Sip Bryson: A Man of Few Words
Beta/Scotts Creek

When slavery ended, the former slaves in Jackson County continued to worship with their former masters. One of these was Sip Bryson, who belonged to one of the white Bryson families living in Beta. Along with several other former Bryson slaves, he attended Scotts Creek Baptist. Now he and the others desired to establish their own house of worship.

Very little is known about Sip and the other founders of Scotts Creek Liberty Baptist Church. All the former slaves apparently belonged to Daniel Bryson and his family, who came into the area in the early 1800's. The elder Daniel Bryson came across Balsam with 140 slaves. However, by 1860, the Bryson families were down to 45 slaves. Daniel Bryson held 21 African slaves, while Daniel G. Bryson had eight, Thaddeus D. Bryson had 15 and William Hamilton Bryson, Jr. had one.

Which one of these families owned Sip is unknown. The other former slaves were Moses, Ella, Betsy, Sylvia, Rena, Abby and Elizabeth Bryson with Lucinda Bryson Love and Dorcus Love. Since the first location of the newly formed African American Scotts Creek Liberty Baptist Church was on Colonel Bryson's farm, it's apparent the slaves belong to the colonel.

Now free, the former slaves had to provide for themselves. It is said Sip Bryson stayed around the Brysons' who held him in slavery. When the daughter of the family married a Waycaster and moved to Dark Ridge, Sip decided he wanted to visit them. It was apparent he told everyone that he was going to Dark Ridge to visit the Waycaster children.

Trying to convince Sip that the trip was impossible fell on deaf

ears. A journey to Dark Ridge was too far away for someone who
had no means of transportation or any money. His folks tried to tell
him that the journey was impossible, Sip didn't argue with them. A
silent and determined man, he packed his few belonging. Without any
fanfare, one spring day, he bid his family and friends farewell and
started walking across Balsam. By then, the Western North Carolina
Railroad ran through Balsam and he decided that perhaps he could
hop a train going toward Dark Ridge. He felt that he didn't need any
money. Now all he had to do was find the train and steal away on it.

The next morning both black and white began a manhunt. Going
to Dark Ridge was a foolish notion and the searchers were afraid he
might have fallen in the water. They started the search from Colonel
Bryson's home and headed toward the woods. They knew Sip was
barefooted, because he didn't like shoes. As they tramped through
the woods, they called his name.

They searched the woods, but Sip could not be found. They
feared Sip had died or was dying. However, on the third day as they
approached the stream, they found Sip sitting on the bank of the
stream with his feet dangling in the cool water .

One of the searchers asked, "Sip, didn't you hear us?"

"Sip is man of few words and hollers at no man," he said.

The folks bought Sip back to Colonel Bryson's home. The bottom
of his feet were blooding from tramping through the woods in the
shadow of night. Although, he walked barefooted all the time, the
tangled woods pierced his hardened, cracked feet.

Sip Bryson was a loyal servant who wanted to see the children of
his former master. Being a chartered member of the Scotts Creek Liberty Baptist Church, he was a devoted Christian. And perhaps because
Sip was a man of few words and hollered at no man, this made him
invisible as he quietly worshipped God without any fanfare.

Within the white community of Scotts Creek, Sip's words became a legend. "Sip is a man of few words and hollered at no man."

George Rogers: First African American Land Owner
Long Branch

When the Civil War began, George Rogers was the slave of David Rogers. He was the most highly valued slave at $1050 dollars when David inherited him from his father's estate in 1855. Along with George, young David got George's mother and two of his younger siblings.

During those years before the war, George learned the art of tanning. He started curing hides and leather, which he made into harnesses, bridles and other leather goods needed on the farm. The farm was just over the hill from the county seat of Webster.

By mastering the craft of tanning, he did jobs for other farmers in the surrounding area. With his earning, George got ten per cent and David kept 90 per cent. He could save it or purchase something for his family.

On July 11, 1861, everything changed. David Rogers was going to war. The Southern states had separated themselves from the Northern states. Without hesitating, David Rogers mounted his horse and headed out to fight the Yankees. He left his mother Polly in the care of George and his mother Harriet. With David gone, it meant more work for the four remaining slaves.

By April 1863, there were rumors the war was over and the slaves had been emancipated. That meant George and his family were free to leave the farm and he could seek his own fortune. After all, he was an excellent tanner. Being treated almost like a son, he felt he had an obligation to David and his mother who was on her deathbed. He had promised Master David that he would take care of his mother and his farm until he returned from the war.

Therefore, George remained on the farm, continuing to care for his master's mother. With the money he made from applying his tanning skills, he could support his family. He tanned hides and made leather goods

Late in May, Polly Rogers died. When her sons and daughters gathered for the funeral, David still was away at war. They had not heard from him since October 1861 and the family feared that he was dead.

Now a decision had to be made. Since David was not married, his siblings allowed George, Harriet, Lewis, and Louisa to continue to run the farm. Harriet took care of the house, while George, Lewis and Louisa worked the farm. Patiently, they waited. Polly was laid to rest in the family cemetery.

For the next two years, George and his mother, Harriet, managed the farm as though it was their own. Living on a farm produced food, but still life was difficult. Most people could not afford to pay for George's tanning services, therefore they bartered with anything to eat or drink.

Finally, in April 1865, the news spread quickly through mountains that the war had ended with General Robert E. Lee's surrender to General Ulysses S. Grant in Virginia. Before they could understand what freedom meant, news of Lincoln's death came.

For most slaves, they wondered what all this meant. Harriet and George worried that the other Rogers would throw them off the place with the news of war being over. George knew that there was no one around the area who could pay them to work. Therefore, George made the decision once more to stay.

On September 1, 1865, David Rogers came home. He had been a prisoner of war for five long years. He was surprised to see George and his family had remained on the place. They were free and could go anywhere they wanted. However, George was a faithful slave who had kept his master's homestead going while Master David went to fight a war.

David Rogers was broke, but he allowed George and his family to remain on the farm. Together, they put their lives back on a good economic base. Being a skilled tanner, George continued to do that in his spare time. Since George was using David's tools, anything that George created and sold, they split the profit.

However, George had made another request. He asked David could he and his family use Rogers as their last name. David Rogers granted George's request as long as he did not disgrace the Rogers' name.

On May 24, 1872 George bought land from W. P. Wood and his wife Jane for $450. By then, he had married Eliza and had several children. Therefore, George built a house to accommodate his growing family, which included his mother. He was one of the first former slaves to own land in Jackson County.

Afterwards, Eliza had more children. When their son, James, died at three, she was heartbroken. In 1879, she died and few years later, George married young Josephine Gibbs, and his family continued to grow. He had about twenty-three children from his marriages and his extra marital affairs.

On August 24, 1912, George passed away. The former slave had been a farmer, a tanner, and a landowner. He left his family economically well off.

Lucinda Bryson Love:
The First Legal Marriage after the Civil War
River View

Seven months after the Civil War, Lucinda Lou Bryson married Joe Marion Love. In Jackson County, their marriage became the first legal union for a black couple after the emancipation. They were married in November 1865. From this union, there were six children.

During slavery, most slave marriages were not legal. The master of the slaves or the masters of the slaves gave the couple the right to "Jump the Broom." By jumping the broom, the slaves were considered a marriage couple. Sometimes the slaves would belong to the same slave owner or two slaves met each other through slave owners' social life.

At any rate, the slave marriage was a benefit to the owner who held the female slave. All the children born of that marriage would belong to him. This meant he could sale them, if he wished to do so. Lucinda (Cindy) appeared to have been produced through such an arrangement when she was born on February 25, 1846. Colonel Thaddeus D. Bryson bought Cindy at the tender year of four. When she died, her parents were unknown to her surviving relatives.

After the Civil War, each state required that a slave couple obtain marriage license, go before a justice of the peace, and repeat their marriage vows. By repeating their vows before a justice of the peace and putting an X on a marriage certificate, their union would be legal. Now they were no longer living in sin, nor were they chattel property. The slaves became a legal citizen of the United States of America.

Lucinda Lou "Cindy" Bryson was a slave of Colonel Thaddeus Bryson of Jackson County. In 1850 the colonel purchased her for $450. She remained in the Bryson household until the conclusion of the Civil War. Whether Joe and Cindy jumped the broom during the Antebellum South is not known. Colonel Bryson gave the couple acres of mountainous terrain in Dillsboro in the district called River View, where most blacks were settling. They made their home there and raised a family.

In 1871 Lucinda Love along with other black members of the Scotts Creek Baptist Church requested permission to establish their own church. In May the white church granted letters to several Brysons and Loves to establish their own place of worship. With of the help of the mother church, the church was organized. The first location was a log cabin on the upper part of Colonel Daniel G. Bryson's farm, near the gum springs.

Mrs. Cindy served her church until she died July 1947.

She observed her 101st birthday six months before her death. When she died, she had outlived all her neuter family, except a daughter, Rose. However, grandchildren and great-grandchildren survived her.

The land that Colonel Bryson deeded to Cindy is now in the hands of Jackson County. The water treatment plant occupied the bottom part of the land.

The Incident at Dillsboro Crossing
(FINDING A PLACE TO WORSHIP)
Dillsboro

Before the Civil War, a few blacks officially joined their masters' churches. In the newly formed Mt. Pleasant Baptist in 1852, a black sister joined. This church is located in the Balsam area. About ten miles down the road in Webster, the Webster Baptist Church included eight colored members in 1853. Therefore, after the Civil War, most former slaves continued to worship with their former owners.

In 1871, the Scotts Creek Baptist, a predominant white church, received a letter from former slaves asking permission to establish their own church. With permission granted, Scotts Creek Liberty Baptist Church was organized. The former slaves met in a log cabin on the upper part of Colonel Daniel G. Bryson's farm, near the gum springs, which is also near Billy Ray Bryson's home.

Just over the hill, in the other scattered black communities, there were no organized churches, although Mr. Jim Wells stated that the black Webster Baptist Church was the first black church in the county. They worshiped with their former masters, or found a place to worship by inviting black ministers from out of town to speak at their Sunday morning gathering.

In June 1892 in Dillsboro, there was no church building for the blacks nor the whites. Therefore, the public school building was used for an occasional public worship by all denominations. Up until that point, only white folks used the building. Now the black folks of Dillsboro sought permission to use the structure, which was located just across the creek in a little cove near the railroad. They applied to Dr. J. M. Candler and S. P. Conner of the school committee. Permission was granted for the black folks to occupy the building for one night.

A colored evangelist from Asheville was going to preach. Evangelist John Garrett was a well-known preacher of the Gospel and most colored folks in the county wanted to hear him. Therefore, most everyone in the flatland of the county knew he was coming and where he was going to be. This included blacks and whites.

On the night of the event, songs of praise came from the white school building. Anyone who heard the music recognized the melody as being a black one. Although the white churches in the area were not stiff and dry in their approach to Sunday worship, this was black music.

The school building was a two-story structure with an auditorium was on the bottom floor. The black population dressed their Sunday best came from just over the hill to Dillsboro to hear the renowned Evangelist John Garrett preach. They came from Sylva, Balsam, Montieth Gap, Hog Rock, Peter's Bluff, and Long Branch to get a spiritual blessing for the week. Some walked. Others rode horses, while others came in horses and buggies.

A gathering of black folks in a white establishment did not set well with some of the local white folks. As Rev Garrett began to preach there were shouts and rocks tossed at the upstairs windows. There was some uneasiness among the congregation, but the service continued. If they ignored the assault, the perpetrators would go away.

However, that was not the case. The angry mob circled the building and fired volley of stones through the windows. The shattering glass sprayed the room. Several of the congregations were struck by shattered window glass. There were no serious injuries, just damage to the school. Racial comments were made and the gathering decided it was time to go home. Under the cover of darkness, the congregation disbursed, when they felt that the perpetrators had left. They did not wait around for another attack. Someone could be seriously injured.

They reported the incident. However, the local High Sheriff did nothing about it. Rev. Garrett reported it to Asheville. Detective Deaver came to Dillsboro and investigated the situation. Deaver arrested the perpetrator John Spence, who was from Buncombe County, but he had trouble getting him arraigned. Spence was a carpenter and employed by J. J. Mason, the Marshal of the town.

It seemed that no magistrate would arraign until he was brought before Justice J. W. Buchanan. However, after the examination of several black witnesses, Justice Buchanan deemed that the evidence was insufficient and the charges were dismissed.

Shortly afterward, Spence was rearrested on the same charges issued by Squire A. M. Parker of Sylva, but again the charges were dismissed. After all, he was just a good old boy protecting what was his.

Now the lines were drawn. Blacks had to find their own building to worship. With the help of prominent whites, the Blacks were able to obtain property to build their own sanctuaries. Most black churches in Jackson County obtained their land from prominent white citizens with the stipulation that the land be used for church only or it would return to the owner.

African American Liberty Baptist Church

Aunt Zelia and Son: Pillars of their Church
River View

Mr. and Mrs. Major W. Wells lived in the River View community of Jackson. According to the 1900 century census, there were six people in their household. Major W. Wells, a farmer, headed the household. His wife, Zela, (Zelia) J. worked as a hotel cook. Being in the black community of Dillsboro, she probably worked at Mount Beulah Hotel in downtown Dillsboro. Today Mount Beulah is still open, but has been renamed the Jarrett House. It was named Mount Beulah for the founder of Dillsboro William Dills' daughter.

The children in the household were Mary M. and James W. Also listed were a granddaughter, Gertrude and a great-grandson, Regional who was three years old. Gertrude was fifteen. Mary was twenty-one and worked as cook. Seventeen years old, James worked as Tannery laborer.

Mr. Major was illiterate, but he always pretended he could read. Usually, the page he was "reading" was turned upside down. He was a proud man. Although he could not read, he knew how to figure. Born in 1839 in North Carolina, Mr. Major was perhaps a slave from the eastern part of the state. Coming to the mountains after the Civil War, he felt free.

Mrs. Zelia was born about 1858. Her mother's name is unknown, but her father was Bus Van Hook. She was born Arzelia Jane Van Hook in Macon County.

The couple probably met in Macon County, made their way to Jackson County, and settled on the banks of the TuckaseigeeRiver in the Dillsboro area. They bought mountainous acres of land and built a two-story house overlooking the river. They had six children, but according to the 1900 census report, three children had died.

Mr. Major planted an orchard on the hill above his home. From the hilly land, he was able to make a garden to keep his family from starving.

Mrs. Arzelia heard of the black Webster Baptist Church just over the hill. Therefore, on Sunday morning, with her children and grand-children, she walked to Webster to the little white frame church in the wilderness. The black folks who belonged to the church told them it was first black church in the county.

On the way home from church, they walked with the other black folks from River View. As they traveled back home, they talked about erecting a church in their community. There were enough families to establish one. They would not have to travel just over the hill. How-ever, they continued to go to Webster Baptist Church and became members.

On June 8, 1914, M. Y. Jarrett, justice of the Peace of Jackson County recorded the sale of land for the church. Robert B. Whitmire and his wife sold a plot of land to James Whitmire, M. W. Wells and Cudge Thomas, the Trusties of River View Baptist Church for ten dol-lars. It was adjoining the lands of Robert Whitmire and River View School.

It is quite evident that on Sundays the school serviced as the church while they built the plank structure. That meant they no longer had to travel to Webster for worship. In August 1928, the church reported to the Waynesville Baptist Association that there were eighteens members (4 males and 14 females).

Six years later, Mr. Major died. By 1936 Cudge Thomas and Robert Whitmire were dead. This left his son, Mr. Jim Wells, to step in and try to keep the church going. He moved his membership from Webster Baptist Church, but still allowed both churches to worship to-gether. Thus, the Feast in the Wilderness was created.

Mr. Jim now worked in Sylva Supply, the company store of the Tannery. He was not in the main building, but he handled the produce downstairs. People brought the produce in or they could buy produce. With this job, Mr. Jim met many white folks. Being a talkative man, Mr. Jim told them about his church.

By 1940, the members saw that they needed a new building. It was also the time that many blacks migrated north. The building funds were not enough to build a church. Although Mrs. Zelia had retired from the hotel, she was not idle. Walking from Dillsboro to Sylva, she solicited money from Dillsboro and Sylva businesses for the building fund. She persisted and she usually got donations.

It would take them about four years before River View Baptist had a new church. The pulpit furniture was mahogany as well as matching pews. Instead of building a plank sstructure, theyerected a brick one. The tiny little church was beautiful as it sat on a knoll, which looked over the TuckaseigeeRiver in the River View African American community.

When the flood waters of 1940 swept through Jackson County, Mrs. Zelia left her home for higher ground. She found shelter in her son's home that sat on a higher knoll then hers, just a few feet away. As the river continued to rise, she wanted to save her upright self-playing piano. At that time, Eloise, her granddaughter and her husband Lee Roy Casey stayed there. With all the excitement, Uncle Lee Roy and Mr. Jim moved the piano to higher ground. When the flood was over and the Tuckaseigee had receded, it took six men to put Mrs. Zelia's piano back in her home.

On January 16, 1959, Mrs. Zelia passed away. Together, Mrs. Zelia and her husband had accomplished many things. Although Mr. Major could not read and write, his children and grandchildren obtained an education.

Mr. Jim continued to attempt to keep the church door open. It was a difficult task; because most people were leaving the small imitate black community of River View. By the early 1960's, there was perhaps three families still living there. Those families had no children to keep the church going. They had left for a better future. Even Mr. Jim's children moved away after they obtained an education. There was nothing here in Jackson County for them. A move to Asheville was a big step and most did.

Mr. Jim and his wife, Mrs. Katherine, moved to Asheville in 1971. River View Baptist permanently closed its door. Now the River View Baptist Church is an empty shell, setting majesty on the hill. Inside, there is nothing. The  pews and the pulpit furniture are gone. However, the memories linger in the minds of those that are alive to remember.

Integrated Service at Riverside Baptist Church
Webster

Webster was the hub of activities after the Civil War. Shortly before the war, Jackson County was created with Webster as the county seat. In the later 1880's the black citizens of Webster, who were once slaves, organized their own church. It was located around Buchanan's Loop. Today, the church no longer exits. In the beginning it was officially consecrated as Riverside Baptist Church, but it was called Webster Nigger Baptist by some. Although there is no official record of the name of the church, there was an old hymn book found in the building that had Riverside Baptist written on the inside cover of the book. Mr. Jim Wells also stated that the first black church in the county was Riverside, so there are excellent reasons to believe that is the truth.

This entry is in the minutes of what is now Cullowhee Baptist recorded before and after the Civil War:

"Blacks were early members of the church. Coming as converts in 1824 were black Bob, black Jude and black Sookey. The latter was the handmaid of James B. Love. In 1827 black Dinnah joined as a convert. After the Civil War black members left to join a church of their own."

One has to remember that Webster was the county seat. Therefore, the former slaves found jobs in the area. On Hog Rock, a mica mine employed both black and white miners. A hotel and boarding houses were there to house the people who had business at the County Courthouse. Black women were washerwomen, who did white folks' laundry. Webster was a growing little village as the hub of the county's business settled there. White folks came down from the mountains when court was in session. Therefore, they stayed at the boarding house or the hotel.

With black and white coexisting, it was natural for the black congregation of Webster Black Baptist Church to invite the white residents of the village for one of their special services. One of those services took place on a fifth Sunday and one of the early Feast in the Wilderness. Mary Morris recalled they carried flowers for their relatives' graves, who were buried in the nearby Webster Cemetery. Like a Sunday morning parade, the white folks walked the dusty red clay road to the black church. Leading the parade were Professor Robert Madison and Professor Oliver. These two white educators were the guest speakers.

Mr. Jim Wells presided over the service. Apparently, during the devotional service, the Holy Ghost spirit touched Mr. Jim's soul and he began to shout. Frightened by the outpouring of the Holy Spirit, Mary's brothers, Jack and Tom Morris bolted over the back pews and ran home. Other white young boys, like Dale Coward, Billy Joe Cowan, Ted Ed Davis, and Tommy Nicholson followed.

Mrs. Florence Fisher, who babysat for the Morris had Mary and Ralphine Nicholson seated beside her. They stared up at Miss Florence, who was clapping her hands and the two little girls did the same. There was no escape for them. The two just sat there and enjoyed the service.

The integrated service at Webster Baptist continued that day. There was the usual morning service and dinner on the ground. Church members bought lots of food like fried chicken, potato salad, green beans, sweetbread and other desserts. All the white folks who attended the meeting were familiar with the black folks cooking because most had prepared meals for them. They knew they were in for a delicious meal.

After eating, the afternoon service began. The black members showed off their musical talent in a short program. Mrs. Florence probably strolled down the aisle as she sang one her favorite hymn. The black children of the church recited poems and sang songs.

When the afternoon service was over, white folks drifted back to their homes. Although they came to together that special Sunday and saw each other practically every day, their social lives hardly ever touched. However, that Sunday in the 1930's, they worshipped together in the little village town of Webster.

Aunt Zettie Casey: Laundering was her Business
Old Settlement

Aunt Zettie, as the white folks knew her, lived in the Old Settlement across the Tuckaseigee River. She was the second wife of Bill Casey. She operated an outdoor laundry from her home on her farm. In other words, she washed clothes for several prominent white families in Webster. Her given name was Rosette, but she was affectionately called Aunt Zettie. She and her step-grandson Henry Casey or her grandson Buster Hyatt drove a horse drawn wagon into the little village of Webster to collect and deliver the laundry to the Lewis Broyles, the Will Cowan's, the Gene Allison's, the Doug Davis' and others.

To the white children, the sight of Aunt Zettie was source of excitement. They ran behind the slow moving wagon. Each child was perhaps anticipating which house Aunt Zettie was going to stop.

As she delivered the clean laundry, she would pick up the dirty laundry. With each family laundry, she was furnished a cake of soap. Most of the soap was Octagon, while others might have a homemade cake of soap for their laundry. Sometimes, Aunt Zettie would use her homemade soap to wash her customers' clothes if there were not enough leftovers. She melted the leftovers and reshaped them.

She used three large black pots to wash the clothes. The first pot was used to wash the clothes, which meant using a washboard to scrub them clean. After that, the clothes were put into another pot of boiling water, which they were stirred with a huge ladle. The third pot was used to rinse the clothes. Before the clothes were put in the third pot, the clothes were taken out and put on a chopping block. With the huge ladle, Aunt Zettie would beat the clothes. This process helped get all the suds out. Rinsing the clothes was also done by hand. The pots sat on a pit fire in the backyard and usually Uncle Henry or Buster maintained it. Aunt Zettie's daughter, Effie, and her grandchildren helped wash the clothes. It was a family business. Mrs. Evelyn Bryson Austin, a great grandchild, stated that they worked from six in the morning to six in the evening. Evelyn and her sisters, Hannah, Hattie Sue and Rose helped with wash as well as carry water and gather the wood for the fire. Her brothers, U. Z. and Walt contributed.

Laundering the clothes meant the clothes had to be dried and pressed. Evelyn and her sisters helped put the clothes on the line and assisted in ironing and folding them.

After washing each family's clothes, there would be a portion of the cake soap left. Aunt Zettie would not use this unused portion for any of the other families. Carefully she put them aside, making sure that they remained separate. Therefore, when she delivered the laundry, she told them that she had enough soap left over for the next week.

It would take all day to wash, press and fold the clothes. It was suppertime when they finished. They had only taken a thirty-minute break to eat dinner at noonday. Everyone was tired, but there was farm work to do before bedtime.

Aunt Zettie was a religious person and member of African American Webster Baptist Church. She supported her church and believed in being honest in her laundry business. When the Depression came, some of Aunt Zettie's friends wanted to know why she did not keep the unused soap. She told them, "When I get up Yonder, I don't want to do no explaining about pieces of soap."

Being in business, Aunt Zettie kept a budget. However, she was no good at figuring money. With all her earning, she went down to Cowan's store to get help from him. When he was not there, she grabbed anyone in the Cowan family to help her. With the help of Helen Cowan, Aunt Zettie counted her money. Mrs. Cowan tells this story: The two of them would divide the money into portions and place them in various colored bits of cloths. The red bundle was for food, the blue bundle was for clothing, the yellow bundle was for taxes, the green bundle for personal spending and a white bundle for the Lord. After tying the bundles, Zettie picked them up and put them in her apron pocket.

Helen picked up the small green bundle.

"Is this bundle for the Lord?"

"No, that is mine." Aunt Zettie put the bundle in pocket. "I work for what I get."

When washing machines with a wringer were invented, Aunt Zettie and other washerwomen were forced out of business. In the old days, Aunt Zettie was a welcome sight. Her hands were rough and strong. With those powerful hands, she could squeeze nearly all the water out of a garment. Then she shook it out and pinned the garment on clothesline, there were no drips of water flooding the ground. Aunt Zettie made sure she did not pop a button off. Occasionally, when she did pop off a button, she sewed it back. Even sometimes, she mended torn garments. Being a religious woman, she hummed and sang hymns and gospel music to help the task and day go by quickly.

In those days, black folks visited each other. Therefore, Aunt Zettie took one day off and went visiting. She took two or three of her grandchildren with her. They walked along the Tuckaseigee River and visited the Rogers, the Casey's, Aunt Clercy and others. She stopped a bit and then went on, making sure, she got back home before dark.

The next day, everyone in the household returned to their chores. When Sunday morning came, they walked to church. They went to Webster Baptist or walked the country mile to River View Baptist.

Mojo: The Healing Hands of Aunt Clercy
Cullowhee

When the Africans were brought to the shores of United States and enslaved by plantation owners, they brought their religion with them. It was one thing to take their identity away, but their religious practices remained deep in their souls. Those slaves who practice their religion, which was healing hands and black magic, most passed the secrets on to their children. Clerissa Love was born in 1877, making her a second generation Negro. In other words, her parents were slaves and passed the healing hands and black magic to her.

At the age of 20, Clerissa Love married William Coward on December 29, 1897. They lived in Cullowhee across the Tuckaseigee River. Their home sat on a bank that seemed to have been dug out just for their homesite.

All her life she held on the old African ways of healing. By the time I was born in 1943, she was 56 years old. As I was growing up, I can remember her coming to my house. She and my mother would sit on the upstairs front porch and talk.

By this time, she was in her early sixties and like most older black women in Jackson County, they never learn to drive; much less own an automobile. Aunt Clercy walked from her house to my house, which was a country mile.

My sister Lorinda would occasionally develop a sty under her eye. This is an infected eyelash follicle, which resembles a boil. They are uncomfortable and can be quite painful. If Lorinda had a sty under her eye, Aunt Clercy always did her "hocus-pocus" on it. She would blow on it and make mysteriously moves with her slim black hands with beautiful long fingers, going across Lorinda's sty about three or four times. Then, she'd blow on Lorinda's eye, and take a small piece of velvet cloth and cover her eye. As she did this, she chanted. The sty did not disappear right away, but it usually would be gone within a few days.

Because the sty did not dissipate, Lorinda commended that Aunt Clercy's healing hands did not work. She felt that her unbelief of Aunt Clercy's healing power prevented the healing.

Other blacks in the Cullowhee area allowed Aunt Clercy to use her healing hands to heal their children from colic or other childhood illness. Rev. Cyritha Rogers West recalled that her mother, Mrs. Ella Mae Rogers, Mr. Will Rogers' daughter-in-law, told her that Aunt Clercy healed her from colic. Colic is cause by gas in the stomach, which causes the tongue to turn white. Aunt Clercy called it baby colicky. Most babies have colic when they are from one to three months old.

One day when Aunt Clercy visited Ella Mae to see the new addition to the Rogers clan, she found Ella Mae rocking Cyritha who was crying.

"I just can't stop her from crying," Ella Mae told Aunt Clercy.

"Let me hold the child," Aunt Clercy replied. Ella Mae handed her to Aunt Clercy.

Gently, she rocked the baby. "You done fed her."

"Yeah," Ella Mae assured. "But she keeps on crying."

Aunt Clercy looked into Cyritha's mouth and saw that her tongue was coated white. "Child, that baby has baby colicky."

"What?"

"It ain't serious, just baby colicky."

Aunt Clercy gently blew into Cyritha's mouth. This blowing into the mouth calmed her and she fell asleep. Gently, Aunt Clercy returned Cyritha to her mother. There are other instances that Aunt Clercy used her healing hands to cure or alleviate pain and suffering from the human body

As a child, Rea Ann recalled her mother, Aunt Clercy and others having a quilting party. When harvest came, Mrs. Ella Mae and Aunt Clercy broke beans together. Gardening was important to Aunt Clercy and to most of the homes in the mountain. They canned and preserved their food for the winter. Aunt Clercy knew about all the old remedies. Like Granny Ede, Aunt Clercy handed down folk remedies, but most are now lost.

Aunt Clercy, not only served the black community, she touched the white community as well. Most all the neighbors around her were white. She made rag dolls for the little girls. She shared her knowledge and wisdom with the women folks. She fed them. Although Aunt Clercy believed in the old ways of healing, church was important too. She was a member of Mt. Zion AME Zion Church in Cullowhee before it moved to its present location.

She saw the church grow and watched as they removed the graves from the College Hill to their permanent resting place.

Like most black folks at that time, Aunt Clercy felt that desecrating a cemetery of graves was sacrilegious, but to bulldoze over them was worse. It was abominable. Not only were there 76 graves, buried was the amputated arm of Tom Love. It needed to remain in the ground or the stub would ache.

A blessing over those graves before removal and a blessing over them after reburial was important. If there were no blessings, their spirits would not rest. A ceremony was held before removal, another was held after all the bodies, and body parts were reburied. Now their spirits rest.

Aunt Clercy (back row third from left) pictured with Mt. Zion congregation in front of the building on College Hill.

Grant Wilson: Backbone of Maize Chapel
Tannery Flats

Mr. Grant G. Wilson was born in North Carolina in about 1876. Being a light skinned African American; he was listed as a Mulatto. That meant that one of his parents was a white person.

According to 1920 census Mr. Grant's parents' birthplace was also North Carolina. Listed on the 1860 slave schedule, a John Wilson owned eight slaves and six of these slaves were listed as Mulattoes. Among them was a 31 year old male who would have been 45 years old when Mr. Grant was born. He also owned a 17-year-old female slave, listed as a mulatto. By the time the Civil War ended, the couple would have been about 36 and 22 years old respectively.

At any rate, Mr. Grant Wilson's parents were born during slavery in Western North Carolina. There were not many free African Americans before the war, although some slave-owners freed their slaves before the war began. Therefore, it a good possibility that his parents were slaves and labored for John Wilson, who was a farmer.

Mr. Grant grew up in the Tannery Flats in the African American Community. He attended the African American one-room school, which was located in the Scotts Creek area of the African American community, which was about a half a mile way.

According to the 1920 Federal Census, he could read and write. This census also recorded that Mr. Grant had married Mary T. (Texas). Now 48 years old, Mr. Grant was working in the Tannery as a piece worker. He owned his home and had raised a son Charles F. who was born on October 23, 1891. Mr. Charles married Bessie Bryson and, like his father, worked for the Tannery, which was just across the creek from the African American community where the Tannery provided homes for his workers.

His name suggest that he was named after General Ulysses S. Grant of the Union army, who accepted General Robert E. Lee's sword when the Confederate army surrendered to end officially end the war at Appomattox.

When the African American Methodist Church was organized in the Tannery Flats, he became a member. The first church house was a wooden structure, which was built in 1914 and named for George Maize, who was the presiding elder of the Asheville District of AME Zion Methodist churches.

Around the early 1940's the plank building was in dire need of repair. Instead of razing the structure, the Trustees, which Mr. Grant was a member decided to erect the new church around the old one.

With plans outlined by another church member, Mr. Dallas Gray, who was a master carpenter and the designer of their sister church Mt. Zion of Cullowhee, the Trustees and pastor, Rev. Keaton approved the plans.

Mr. Wilson Grant continued to serve his church and his community. After his death, his wife, Aunt Texas was a driving force behind Maize Chapel, just as was their son, Mr. Charlie Wilson. The membership was small, but Maize Chapel stayed opened until the early 1990's.

Aunt Mell: Keeper of the Old Ways
Peter's Bluff

Melvinia Coward Chavis was the daughter of Mr. Alfred Coward and Mrs. Eliza Coward. She was born on July 8, 1878 in Cullowhee. Being born only 13 years after the freedom of her parents, Aunt Mell learned to make soap from ashes and lye. She made candles out of bees wax and learned how to make brooms from corn shuck. Her blackberry wine was seasoned just right. Along with Aunt Clercy, she quilted and made roped throw rugs. The two were related by marriage.

Converted at an early age, she joined Mt. Zion AME Zion Methodist Church in Cullowhee. As long as she was able, she served the church. With a willingness to served, she was always ready to do her part. Aunt Mell married twice. Her first husband was Mr. John Rogers, who was part of the Rogers clan. After his death, she married Mr. Charlie Chavis.

When they got married, they built a house on a knoll in Peter's Bluff. While living there, she sold about an acre of land to Estus Casey. She became acquainted with the Estus Casey family, who moved just below them in 1936. My mother, DeRosette Horne Casey was from Asheville and did not know much about country life. She was a city girl.

Aunt Mell served as a midwife for four of DeRosette's last four out of five children. She helped deliver Lorinda, Victor, Floretta and me. When Victor and I were born, everyone thought it was going to be a single birth. I was born first, then Victor was born about five minutes later. At first, they believed Victor to be the afterbirth.

When Floretta was being born, she almost was delivered in a slop jar. Mother thought she had to urinate, but it was her water breaking. Aunt Mel recognized what was going on as Floretta's head moved through the birth canal. She was able to catch her before she drowned in the waste in the slop jar.

After Mr. Charlie Chavis died, Aunt Mell sold the place to Uncle Henry and Aunt Jessie. She went to live in the Scotts Creek community near the Colored Consolidated School. She took care of Mr. Theodore Moore, who a retired tannery worker at his home. When my mother taught piano lessons at Rev. Smith's home, we stayed there after school. We ate a snack of Ritz Crackers and milk and did our homework while waiting for our mother and father to drive us home.

In her old age, Aunt Mel continued to make soap and brew home-made wine until she was unable to do so. After Mr. Theodore died, she resided in Crawford Nursing Home in Canton, just over the hill from Sylva. She departed this life on August 9, 1973 at the age of 95.

Miss Josephine and Mr. Sherman Davis
Locust Creek

On Friday, February 12, 1954-- just two days before Valentine's Day-- Sherman Davis' beloved Josephine died. He sat on the bedside and thought of the times they spent together. He held in his hand the valentine he had planned to give her. Tears came to his eyes and silently they cascaded down his face. The couple had been married for almost fifty years. They had raised and provided educational opportunities for three children.

Josephine Moore was born in Swannanoa in 1888. She and her siblings were educated in the Swannanoa area. Josephine decided to become a teacher. In those days, you could obtain a teacher's certificate right after high school by passing the board. She had graduated from Allen Home. When she got her teacher's certificate, she went to Georgia and taught in a colored one- room school before coming to Cullowhee to teach at the one-room structure on Thomas Davis Hill. The Mt. Zion AME Zion Methodist Church was adjacent to the school; therefore, she became a member of that church.

In 1912, she was teaching at the Colored School in Cullowhee. She was 25 years old and single. Being a single schoolteacher, she had strict rules she had to follow. After dark, it was forbidden to be alone with a male companion.

There were other restrictions and Josephine pondered the problem. Most girls her age were already married and her mother reminded her of that. Her years in Georgia were great, but she had not found a husband. All of the good ones were married.

Briefly she had know a young General Sherman Davis, who was working with the railroad. He left after a lynching in Tiger. Sherman ran from Tiger, Georgia to North Carolina without looking back. When school closed for that year, Josephine left also.

Now back in the mountains of North Carolina perhaps she would find her true love. Going back home to Swannanoa was not the answer. Just over the hill in Cullowhee might change things. Someone had told her there were plenty of eligible bachelors in the area. In Swannanoa, most of the young men were kin. Slavery had destroyed the order of things. This was a fresh start.

Since there were no boarding houses for colored folks, she had to board with a nice Christian family in the area. The colored school committee got her a room in Thomas Davis's household. The Davis' belonged to the Methodist church and would see to it that she attended church every Sunday. For at church was where a single schoolteacher could meet a nice eligible bachelor.

In the Davis' household was a young man. He was Thomas's youngest son Sherman Davis. Working for the railroad, Sherman had come back to the safety of home. When he returned, his father insisted that Sherman continue his education.

Therefore, when Miss Josephine walked into the one-room school on Davis Hill, she was surprised to see Sherman seated among the other multi-age students, which range from the age of eight to 21. From the attendance of the students, it was apparent to Miss Josephine that the colored folks in Cullowhee Valley wanted their children to obtain an education and she was here to teach them.

Miss Josephine found herself teaching some young men and women who were almost her age. Some of the boys were taller than she, but she had command of her class. With the help of the older students, she managed to maintain order. With all the students in the same room, younger students learned from the lessons of the older students.

Not only that, Miss Josephine was smitten by the charm of Sherman Davis. She saw him at school, at church, and at house where she boarded. When he was not in school and "out on the town," he was a sharp dresser. His hair was naturally wavy and he always parted it in the middle. Clean-shaven with that light complexion, Miss Josephine thought he was handsome. Miss Josephine was in love.

Sherman was also smitten with the stately Miss Josephine. He, too, had noticed her at church socials and sometimes, he stayed after school. Under the watchful eye of Sherman's mother Mrs. Lena

Thomas, Miss Josephine and Sherman became an item. Shortly afterward, the couple was married.

Mr. Sherman knew that he would have Miss Josephine buried on Valentine Day. Arrangements had to be made. He would allow his son Frank and his wife Virginia to made the arrangements. Getting up, he phoned Frank and then he left. He drove into Sylva and went to the colored neighborhood, Tannery Flats. He parked his car and looked around. It was quiet for the morning activities had died down.

Folks were at work and he knew that had to open the store. Walking slowly toward Davis Grocer, he thought of Miss Josephine. He bought the store in the middle of Tannery Flats to serve the colored folks who needed an item quickly without having to leave the neighborhood. When folks asked him why he did, he jokingly said, "I brought it to keep my wife out of mischief."

He opened the door and walked in. Standing in the middle of the room, Mr. Sherman remembered the day the store opened. Miss Josephine had been excited. She was happy to be out of the big rambling two-story house on Locust Creek. She loved people and loved to talk. At the store, she was able to do both.

Now she was gone.

On Sunday at 2 p.m. on Valentine Day, Miss Josephine's funeral was held at Mt. Zion. Her pastor, Rev. Oliver and Rev. Joe Smith of Liberty Baptist conducted the service. Her former students were in charge of the flowers. They buried her in the church cemetery.

Mr. Sherman had been a good provider for Miss Josephine and his family. He had worked in the mica mine in Cullowhee, delivered milk for Sunny Brook Diary (PET), the Mead Corporation as a janitor and office boy, and had driven the bus for the consolidated school.

With retirement and Miss Josephine gone, he continued to operate the store until his health failed him. The door was closed and it was never reopened. A few years ago, the town condemned the building and demolished it. Now only a grassy spot covers the place where it stood.

John C. Howell: Order of Odd Fellows
River View/Tannery Flats

John Calhoun Howell spent his entire life in Jackson County where he was widely known by both Appalachian whites and his African American brothers. He was an active member of the Maize Chapel AME Zion Methodist Church and the Tuckasegee Mason Lodge. Like many African American men in the county, he found that church and fraternal organizations elevated their social status among their people and the respect from the white society.

Born on January 26, 1861 to Henry Howell and Rhoda Cochran, he was just a mere infant when the Civil War was fought. His status as a free man or a slave is unknown. Searching through the 1860 Slaveholders Schedule of Jackson County, there was either Howells or Cochran's who owned slaves.

Growing up in Dillsboro on River View road, he probably was educated in the one-room African American school in the area. Most of these one-room African American schools were only in session for about 15 weeks. Because of the economic situation in the county, John found it hard to attend school, and since he helped his father on the farm; thus, his education was limited.

In 1900 John was single and was listed as the head of the household. According to the census report, he was a farmer and lived on 39 acres of land that was mortgaged. Living with him was his sister, Fannie Howell, who was divorced after 5 years of marriage. Also living there were his 10-year-old nephew Harley Love and his 12-year-old niece Lillie Love.

When the 1910 Federal Census was taken, John was married to Ada Laura Mosley with two children. Both John and Ada were listed with an occupation. John was a farmer and Ada was a dressmaker, who worked from her home. The children, James Henry and Charles C. were just babies. James was merely two years old and Charles was six months old.

Living in the household was Lillie M. Love, whose occupation was listed as a cook. Now 22 years old, his niece Lillie was helping out by being a cook at one of the hotels in downtown Dillsboro.

According to the 1910 Federal Census of Jackson County all occupants of the household were born in North Carolina. This information included their parents. Ada Laura Mosley was born in 1871. She was the daughter of Spencer Mosley, but her birth mother was unknown at the time of her death in 1950.

On August 12, 1912, the Howells had another child. His name was William Lawton Howell. Like their father, the boys began their education in the one-room African American school in the River View. Unlike in their father's days, the school was able to remain open longer than the other African American one-room schools in the county. By the time the boys reached the middle grades, they were bused to Sylva at the new consolidated school for all African Americans in the county.

Although the Howells lived in Dillsboro, they traveled the three miles to Tannery Flats to attend church. They were Methodists and the only church in their area was River View Baptist or journey over the hill to Webster Baptist Church.

While attending Maize Chapel, he became acquainted with Mr. Charlie Bryson, his brother Ben, Mr. Alvin Conley, Mr. Lester McDonald, Mr. Grant Wilson, and other men in the Tannery Flats and Scotts Creek communities. Perhaps to unite their communities, they organized the Order of Odd Fellows, which they heard about from African American men who migrated to this area in the 1920's.

In the History of the Grand United Order of Odd Fellows, it had the largest membership of any African American fraternal society in the late 1800's and the early 1900's. It had its beginnings in England and came to the United States in early 1800's as just a white organization. At first, the white Order of Odd Fellows would not issue the African American Odd Fellows a charter. However, Peter Ogden, an African American, a steward on a ship that sailed to the English seaport of Liverpool obtained a charter on March 1, 1843. When he did, the England's Committee commissioned Ogden as its agent to the United States. The white fraternity refused to acknowledge the leadership of an African American. Therefore, the Grand United Lodge became a segregated society for the African American Odd Fellows.

Just over the hill in Waynesville, an African American Odd Fellows (Richard Valley Lodge #3945) was already established in 1896. The order was appealing to another Lodge to help out with a fellow member, Jefferson Turner, who had been stabbed by a white, to donate to the welfare of his family. Therefore, Odd Fellows Lodge was an organization that African American men could join to assist their communities. It was a fraternity which fought for the rights of African Americans.

Along with other African American men in Jackson County, John helped organize a chapter in Jackson County. At one time the fraternity was more visible than any other fraternity in the African American communities across the country. However, by the 1930's their membership had dropped. With the Depression, the decline of the Odd Fellows continued.

With the rise of the African American Masonic fraternity just over the hill in Asheville, John decided that secret order was the direction they should go. With most of the Odd Fellows gone, the African American men in Jackson County joined the Masonic movement and built a Masonic Hall in the heart of African American neighborhood in the Tannery Flats. Like the Odd Fellows, the Masons were a secret society which believed that Ancient Egypt was the birthplace of Masonry and the Nile Valley teachings of measurements and proportions were used in buildings, which were designed to represent the Universe and man's relationship to it. In other words, they symbolized God as the Master Architect.

John joined the Masonic Lodge, along with others. Most were teachers, preachers and other skilled workers. The fraternity was called the Tuckasegee Mason Lodge. As the Odd Fellows, they did benevolent acts of charity to the African American community. In the 1940's and 1950's they sponsored an African American Boy Scout troop.

On April 29, 1953, Mason John Calhoun Howell passed away at the age of 92. Indeed, he was a moving force in the African American community.

Wheeling and Dealing: Mr. Jim Wesley Wells
River View

Mr. Jim Wells was born James Wesley Wells to Major and Zelia Wells, who came to Jackson County after the Civil War. They settled in Dillsboro in the River View area. Just by the flowing Tuckasigee River, Mr. Jim was born on a hot day in July of 1892. He an d his two sisters grew up on the riverbank and went to school at the one-room black school in the area. He married Katherine Love. They had five children, who graduated from high school and then went on to college or a trade school

For forty years, Mr. Jim Wells worked for C. J. Harris at the Sylva Supply. His job was to load and unload the produces that came

 in downstairs. As a youngster, he worked to help his family. Working in the basement of the Sylva Supply, he came in contact with a lot of white folks. It was the time that most white folks called African Americans niggers. Hence,

down through the years, he was called Nigger Jim.

In 1976, an old white woman asked about Nigger Jim. She lived in the Barker's Creek district and perhaps that was the only name she had heard Mr. Jim called. However, to the African Americans, he was Mr. Jim Wells, a pillar of the African American community.

Mr. Jim had an answer for that degrading word, which white folks called an African American. Robert Blanton, who was youth when Mr. Jim worked in the Sylva Supply, told this story about how Mr. Jim handled the issue. It seemed that Robert's family told their children never to use that word. However, he used it when Mr. Jim confronted him about the reason he was sent downstairs to work with him.

Robert had just graduated from high school and obtained his first job at Supply Sylva. One day when he came to work his boss Jim Hasket, manager of the store, told Jim to go get the liver saw. Being a farm boy, Blanton knew there was no liver saw. Therefore, Blanton and Hasket get into an argument. When the barber, Bob Schuler came into the store Hasket asked him about the liver saw, Schuler agreed with Hasket. Reluctantly, Robert left the store in search of the borrowed liver saw. Hasket had told him that it was either at the A&P or Winn Dixie.

When Blanton returned to the Sylva Supply, he was angry and upset. It seemed like it was practical joke to young boys who came to work at the store. He was so upset he couldn't work. The two men laughed at him and he wanted to lash out at them. Instead, Hasket sent him downstairs to work with Mr. Jim.

Angrily, Blanton went downstairs and told Mr. Jim that Hasket sent him down to work with him. As he worked storing Fertilizer bags in the back room, he tossed them with a hefy swing.

Finally, Mr. Jim approached him. "Boy, what's the matter with you?"

"Nothing." Blanton replied and continued to work.

Mr. Jim insisted that Blanton tell him what was wrong. In anger Blanton told Mr. Jim the lie that they told him and in his anger, he said, "They lied like a yellow nigger."

The moment he said it, he hung his head down and went back to work. All that morning, he avoided Mr. Jim. Deep down, he knew he had to apologize to Mr. Jim. Around three o'clock, he approached Mr. Jim and told him that he was sorry for using that word.

Mr. Jim replied, "I ain't no nigger. A nigger is a circular hole at a sawmill."

Proudly, he patted Blanton on the back. "I am an African Negro."

Mr. Jim ended his career at the Sylva Supply when he had a heart attack. The doctor advised him if he continued to lift those heavy bags, he would have another attack.

He, like Mr. Sherman Davis, bought property in the Tannery Flats where the largest contiguous of African American lived. After purchasing about a half an acre of land which adjoined Miss Delia Sheppard's property, he built a two-story building. Upstairs there were three rooms, which he rented out. One of the areas was a Beauty Salon. His youngest son, Walter, became a barber and opened a shop in Asheville. On Monday when the shop was closed, he would come home and used one of the rooms upstairs in his father's building to give the local blacks a professional haircut.

Downstairs, he opened a restaurant, which most African Americans would call a "juke  joint." There was a jukebox, drinks and food. It was a place where the African Americans could come and relax after a hard day's work at the Tannery; especially on a Saturday night after being paid for the week. This was the only place, besides the church, the African Americans could socialize without the white man's interfering.

Through the years, different individuals managed the restaurant. Mr. Lester and his wife Bell McDonald at one time operated the juke joint, and Mr. William Lawton also had the job of running the joint.

Besides the rent from the building, Mr. Jim had a landscaping business. He worked hard to provide for his family. His white house situated on the hill overlooking the Tuckasigee had a small yard and a set of rock steps floating down to the road. Within the bank at right of the steps was a car garage dug into it. Behind the house was an orchard of fruits, which Miss Katherine canned.

Mr. Jim was an African Negro, who was proud of his African heritage and worked hard to provide for his family. On his children's birth certificate, he listed his occupation as a wholesale grocer. He was one of the first African American entrepreneurs in our county.

SECTION II
(1901-1930)

INTRODUCTION

With African Americans settling in their own communities, other African Americans came just over the hill to reside in this mountainous haven. Former masters gave land to their former slaves. Professional African Americans came to help create a viable community. There were master carpenters, brick layers, tannery workers, shoemakers, blacksmiths, rock masons, plumbers, teachers and preachers. With hotels built in each part of the county, chamber maids, washerwomen, and cooks were needed. African Americans filled those positions. Janitors were for the college and other establishments. Migrating from settlement to another, the African Americans built a church and school to serve their community. Some of these communities were combined, but it was clear that the social activities were segregated. Each race had their own community, although just next door a white family resided.

During this time Jim Crow laws were passed as we headed into the 20th century. Separate but equal was the cry. That meant that white and black could not go to the same school or any other public places. And yet, Jackson County had to slim down it school system. Small one-room schools were closed and consolidated with another one-room school near them. For the African Americans, that meant bussing. From Cullowhee to Sylva and any other African American communities in between had to attend Colored Consolidated School in Sylva. Therefore the scattered African American communities became an inclusive one, as they shared their desires to educate their children and make Jackson County a better place to live for their children.

Mr. Homer Rogers: Born to Work
East LaPorte/Long Branch

On November 8, 1901 in the little hamlet of East LaPorte, Mr. William Homer Rogers was born to Mr. Wilson and Mrs. Ivey Coward Rogers. When he was nine years old, his daddy moved the family to Long Branch, which is now called Falling Rock. They made the trek in a covered wagon driven by two horses. With his three sisters and his parents, Homer moved to a farm just outside of Cullowhee, which was on the backside of the Normal School. There Mr. Homer resided for most of his life. The family raised corn, kept chickens, milked cows and plowed to make a garden. It was the turn of the century and it was difficult to keep body and soul together, especially for the newly freed African American.

In the book *Reflection of Mister Homer, A Photographic Essay*, Homer stated he was born to work. He said, "When my mammy and daddy first set about to have me, they must've been studying work… ." And work he did.

The farm produced corn and potatoes which was used to obtained other things, such as sugar and coffee. Homer and his older sister Sarah Josephine (Josie) worked in the field to keep the weeds from choking the crops. It was hard work, but there was always a reward.

After harvesting Mr. Wilson would hitch the horses to the cover wagon loaded with corn and potatoes, and head for the nearest market place. Since he lived closer to South Carolina, he went there to swap his crops for some of those other needed items. Usually, he would take Homer and sister, Josie, with him.

It was an adventure for the two youngsters as they traveled with their father. On these trips to South Carolina, their father told stories and showed them the different herbs and plants nature provided for various sickness. At the marketplace, Homer and Josie were amazed at the crowd of people and their homes.

Before they returned home Mr. Wilson bought something for his children and his wife, Mrs. Ivey. The two little girls always eagerly awaited their return to see what goodies their father bought them.

Living in the Cullowhee Colored School District, Homer and his siblings attended the one-room school just over the hill in Cullowhee.

However, Homer found friends in both worlds as did most folks in this mountainous region. He realized that sometimes friendship was severed because of their parents' belief. In *Reflection,* he stated, "As long as the babies were in diapers, it was okay for'em to crawl around with the little black babies, but as soon as the white babies were old enough, their folks would whip those diapers off and say, 'Now you stay away from those niggers!'"

Very early, Homer learned to drink corn liquor. It seemed his father made it pure from the corn left over from the harvest. It was pure corn liquor and sometimes he would give Homer a little spoonful. It seemed that Mr. Homer drank daily and he suggested that was the reason he held up so good.

His mother died of kidney failure in her fifties. His father had "sugar" (back then, that's what they called a diabetic). While trying to trim his toe nails, he accidentallly cut his little toe. It wouldn't heal; therefore the doctor had removed his left leg. Now he had to have a shot each day. Homer watched his father suffer through the pain until he died eight years later.

As a heavy drinker, Homer led a jolly life while going about his work. He never married, but he did father some children. Sometimes he would find himself in a fight because of his drinking.

It was the afternoon of August 17, 1951 when Daniel Hooper spent the afternoon at the Rogers' residence. He and Mr. Homer were drinking, talking and arguing, when the conversation turned into a brawl between the two men. It seemed they were going to wreck the house; therefore Homer's father, who was now confounded to a wheel chair, ordered them out of the house.

Angrily Homer left first by the way of the back door. Realizing his mistake, Daniel asked forgiveness and staggered out the front door. As he walked toward his home, a single shot echoed through the air. Instantly Daniel fell to the ground. According to the death certificate he was shot in left side over the heart and the left shoulder.

Homer was arrested for the murder and on October 8, the grand jury returned a true bill of indictment, charging Mr. Homer Rogers with murder in the first degree. In court, Mr. Homer didn't deny the charges, but his lawyer got the charges reduced to manslaughter. He was released from jail where he attempted to put his affairs in order.

When he reported back to court on December 15, he was sentenced to two years on the road with the State Highway and Public

Works Commission. This meant that Mr. Homer Rogers became a member of the chain gang. These convicted felonies slaved, building

roads for public transportation. Chains were worn constantly and only a blacksmith could remove them.

After he served his time, Mr. Homer returned to Long Branch and continued to work the land. While in the field, he thought about his life. He still felt like a young man. However, as he grew older, his eyesight began to fail him...and yet he continued to work the fields. He knew every inch of his land and walked around without stumbling.

During the winter of 1977, Mr. William Homer Rogers had to be hospitalized to be treated for metastasis in his chest and a year later on December 16, he died of cancer of the lungs.

Homer's life was not in vain. Living just a hop and skip from Western Carolina University and dwelling among some WCU's personal, he became acquainted with some of the students and professors. Professor Jim Smythe, an art instructor, used Homer as a model in his advance art classes. An art student and photographer, Will McIntyre, became friends with Mr. Homer and his sister, Miss Josie. From that friendship McIntyre published a photographic essay on Mr. Homer.

Mr. Homer Rogers, who believed in God and that your Christian denomination didn't matter, said, "God's knows heaven...."

Serving in the White Man's War: Pvt. William Rogers
Montieth Gap

Between 1914 and 1917, European countries were at war with each other. The United States tried to remain neutral with Woodrow Wilson leading the country. However, when a secret telegram from Germany foreign minister was sent to German minister in Mexico promising to reward that country a vast area of Southwestern United States in return for Mexican support against the Americans, on April 6, 1917, the United States declared war on Germany. By May 18, the United States passed the Selective Service Act, which empowered the Federal Government to draft men into the armed forces.

In the rush to enlist individuals for combat, President Wilson said that it was a white man's war. However, Dubois asked Black Americans to support the war anyway we could. In other words, Black America had to put aside their prejudices and serve their country whether at home or in the military overseas.

Snuggled in the little hamlet of Montieth Gap in Jackson County in the mountainous area of North Carolina, lived the Lewis Lemuel Rogers family. Mr. Rogers' mother Harriet was a slave of Hugh Rogers. He had married Catherine Gibbs and had several children.

Their second son, William Henry Rufus Garfield Rogers was tall strapping 23 year-old young man who was working at the mica mine on Long Branch. William did not attempt to join the army. He was busy working at the mica mine and helping his father farm the huge acres to feed the family. He attended the one-room black school on College Hill next to the Mount Zion AME Zion Church where he was a member.

Between April and June, North Carolina had not filled their quo of men for the armed forces. Therefore, on June 1, Governor T. W. Bickett appealed to the young men between the ages of 21 to 31 of the state to report to their various recruiting stations to volunteer their service.

Jackson County's young men answered the call and 1069 registered. 45 volunteers were African Americans from four of the fifteen townships. In the Cullowhee Township, 15 African Americans volun-

teered and among them were William and his older brother 26 year-old, Arthur Hamilton. With the other black young men in the county, they left the farm to defend their country.

For the first time in his life, William left the security of home and ventured into another world. He left the mountain and went to basic training. His army photo showed a young man who was apprehensive of the future ahead. After basic training, he was shipped to Wisconsin where he worked on the army base. At that time, most African Americans were not allowed to fight, but remained stateside and help build structures at the camp they were assigned.

380,000 African Americans served their country in this Great War. 200,000 were shipped overseas. Some Black unit fought, but others built bridges, roads, and trenches, which were imperative to the white combat troops Pvt. Rogers went to Camp McCoy in Wisconsin. At home in the mountains of North Carolina it was cold, but winter came early in Wisconsin. The cold winter in Montieth Gap was no match to snow that covered the ground all winter in Wisconsin. All together 8,000 African American soldiers worked there. They lived in tents, which added to the coldness that ran through Pvt. Rogers' bones. He desperately wanted to get back home.

Upon arriving at Camp McCoy, Pvt. Rogers saw that constructions had begun. He noticed that the black troops and white troops were segregated. They lived in separate units and ate in separate dining halls. The African American soldiers built barracks, mess halls, open-sided stables and storage facilities at the base, while most of the white troops trained in field artillery. Where he worked on Long Branch, black and white worked side by side in the Mica Mine. William saw field artillery unit shipped oversea to fight. None of the 8,000 African American troops did.

When World War I ended with an armistice on November 11,

1918, the 8,000 African American soldiers were honorable discharged and sent home. The journey home was not a good one. All Pvt. Rogers wanted to do was to get there safely. All around the country, Black soldiers were being lynched if they crossed a white man.

He befriended a white soldier who helped him out when they crossed the Mason-Dixie line. It was a good thing, for the closer to home he traveled, segregation slapped him in the face. In each southern town, there was a black section in the depot and a white section. Pvt. Rogers realized that he could not go into any restaurant to eat. The white soldier purchased food for him and brought it out to him. Along the journey to his haven, he also realized there were separate facilities in every hamlet they stopped.

After World War I, Pvt. Rogers put away his uniform and picked up his life. Through the church conferences, he met Kathy Estella Love of Waynesville. He courted her and they were married in 1922. He brought his bride to the family home in Montieth Gap. When his father died in 1933, he took over the family farm. His older brother, Ham died in 1925. His mother known in the community as Aunt Kate remained at the homestead until she died in the 1950's. Both races respected her.

By that time, William and Stella had four children and feeding them required more than the land could yield. Therefore, Will went to work for Hester and Afee Construction contractors as unskilled laborer. His years in the army taught him some carpentry skills and William put them to work. These contractors were constructing buildings on Western Carolina Teachers College campus. The college had just purchased the land were the black Methodist church and cemetery was located.

Mr. Will helped lay the bricks. He mixed mortar and carried bricks. In 1927 a white mason, Russell Painter taught Mr. Will how to lay bricks. After Hester and Afee Construction Contractors left, Mr. Will remained in Cullowhee. Armed with knowledge of laying bricks, he began his career as a mason. He fed his family

Although Pvt. William Rufus Garfield Rogers did not fight in combat overseas, he fought a battle of discrimination in his own country. Woodrow Wilson helped set the tone by stating that the war was a white man's war. To some African American soldiers who were restricted to manual labor on an army base, it appeared that it was just another form of slave labor.

Architect of Methodist Churches: George Dallas Gray
Dillsboro

Who was Dallas Gray? George Dallas Gray, a black man who had the skill to design and build churches, was born December 3, 1869 four years after the Civil War. Therefore, Mr. Dallas was not a slave, but perhaps his parents were under bondage. He was born in Franklin to John and Avaline Dehart Gray. He made his home in Dillsboro after marrying Sallie Patton who was 18 years his junior. They had eight children. Mr. Dallas Gray not only an architect, he was also an undertaker for the black community. He built wooden coffins for the decreased and planned the burial for the family. On Mr. Cudge Thomas's death certificate, Mr. Gray was listed as the undertaker.

In 1928, the congregation of Mt. Zion AME Zion Church was in a legal battle with Western Carolina Teachers College (WCTC). WCTC wanted the land in which the church stood along with the empty building of the black one-room school. More important were the seventy-six graves in the adjoining cemetery.

Rumor had it that WCTC was going to bulldoze the graves and build on them. However, WCTC assured the black community that they have the opportunity to dig them up and rebury them in a cemetery where Mt Zion was going to relocate their church.

With the reassurance from WCTC about the graves, the next step was to decide who would design and build the church. The church did not have money to hire an architectural firm to design the building nor did they have money to hire a crew to build it. The old building could not be moved and the design was not modern. It was 1928, not 1892, when the old building was erected.

Within the congregation there were carpenters, repair people and masons who could get the work done. First, they needed a plan. Therefore, from their sister church in the Tannery Flats, they called on Dallas Gray. He was a master carpenter and had designed his own house. Perhaps, he could design the church.

Mr. Dallas accepted the task. He drew up the plans and Mt. Zion's trustees accepted them. The drawing consisted of a sanctuary and a vestibule with a belfry. The foundation was brick with a corner stone placed near the entrance of the church, which was reached by cement steps. The building would be a wood frame.

With the help of the community, Dallas Gray orchestrated the project. The church stands in the shadow of near Western Carolina University located just over the hill.

Years later, Dallas Gray got the opportunity to design and build his home church in the Tannery Flats. The white frame plank building was falling apart. The building had been there since the early 1900s when black folks from the Webster area came to Sylva in search of jobs. Since it was too far them to walk to the Savannah Community to their church, Black Branch Methodist Church, they established a Methodist church in their community. The members purchased land from J. R and Ida E. Love to erect this new church. They completed the church in 1914 and named it Maize Chapel AME Zion Methodist Church for the seated presiding elder, George Maize.

Now in the early 1940's the church needed a new structure. Dallas designed the church with a steep roof and a very high ceiling. The church would be high off the ground with concert steps leading into the building. Instead of a brick or plank structure, the church was built with concert blocks. There was no belfry for the huge bell that hung in the old church. A concert block was built and the bell was bolted to it. Within the concert block, they cemented the original corner stone. Rev. A. D. Keaton, the pastor and the trustees decided to build the new church around the old one.

With the lack of membership due to migration and death, Maize Chapel closed its doors in the early 1980's. The church remained the property of the Blue Ridge Conference until it was bought by Bishop Adam West in 1987. It reopened its doors as God's Holy Tabernacle in 1988.

Built in the 1890s

Built by Dallas Gray in 1929

The Man of the Hour: 'Fessor Davis
Webster

In 1919, the county attempted to consolidate the black one-room schools in the county. With Sylva having the highest population of African Americans, the school board and Superintendent R. L. Madison decided that Sylva would be the location of the consolidated black school. There were three one-room black schools in the small hamlets. In Webster, John Davis was listed as the teacher in the Annual Report of the Public Schools of Jackson County. Since he was the only Black male teacher in the county, he became the principal of the Colored Consolidated School.

Although Davis was hired as the principal of Colored Consolidated School, his wife Carrie was actually the principal of the small one-room black school in Webster, which was the county seat at that time. She was able to find funds to keep the school open beyond the prescribed time of four months the county allowed. Parents from Cullowhee sent their children to attend the school after theirs closed. Some students resided with relatives in the area and perhaps paid the school for their attendance.

John H. Davis and his sister Mattie J. Davis came to the county at the turn of the century. They were born in Rockingham County in the township of Reidsville, North Carolina. Miss Mattie also a teacher, taught in the school system.

John met a local girl, Carrie Love, and married. Like Davis, she was teacher, also. Together Carrie and John opened the one-room school in Webster to service the black children of the area.

John was also a preacher. He never pastored like most Africa American male teachers during this time. He joined Scotts Creek Liberty Baptist Church in Sylva. Being a prominent member of the African American community, he became a deacon. Along with his deaconship, Rev. Davis joined the Sacred Order of the Mason and reached the highest order in that African American organization, which served most of Western North Carolina.

Being a member of this organization further elevated his status in the African American community. Therefore, Rev. John Davis was looked upon in both black and white communities with respect. This respectability allowed the white school board to appoint him as principal, although his wife was perhaps more qualified.

From the union of John Davis and Carrie Love were five chil-

dren. Their son Ralph followed in his parents footsteps and became a teacher. He joined the faculty of Colored Consolidated School as a science teacher.

After his father retired, most blacks in the Sylva area wanted Ralph as the next principal, but the board went outside the county to hire the next principal.

Rev. John H. Davis had brought the black students into the twentieth century. From 1919 to 1942, he held the job of principal at Colored Consolidated School.

After his retirement, John and his wife returned to Reidsville. He had made his mark on the African American history of Jackson County, because he was the man of the hour.

In the Liberty Baptist 100th Anniversary booklet, Rev. Davis is listed with "Gospel Sons of Liberty Baptist Church" along with eight other members who were preachers.

For a Grammar School Diploma: George Estus Casey
Cullowhee/Sylva

On April 21, 1928 at Jackson County Colored Consolidated School, Estes (Estus) Casey was awarded his eighth grade diploma. Estus was born on May 2, 1908 to Mr. George and Mrs. Sadie Hooper Casey. They lived in the Cullowhee area. Being the son of George, he worked hard to help his father feed the family. There were eight boys and one girl and Estus was the second oldest son.

However, his mother, Sadie was an advocate of education. Her father being a product of slavery, she knew well that to get ahead in life, a good education was important. Estus' older brother Henry had attended A&T College in Greensboro, North Carolina two years earlier. It was his mother's desire that all their children be educated. She had saved up egg money to do it.

Tragedy occurred in 1926. During childbirth, Sadie died. Henry was at A&T when his mother died. He came home, but he didn't return because his father had taken the money for his education and spent it perhaps on Sadie's funeral. Upset, Henry left and went to live with his grandfather and his wife.

Estus remained at home. When school was in session, Estus sometimes didn't attend because his father hired him out to work for white farmers or to go with his dad to help him shoe horses in the mountainous regions of Cullowhee.

With the little one-room school only being 15 weeks, it was difficult for Estus to keep up with the students his age. Starting to school about the age of seven, it took him about 13 years to obtain his grammar school diploma. However, there were other conflicts. In 1921, the county consolidated all the county's colored one-room schools. Cullowhee Colored School Committee refused to send their students to the school, which was located about seven miles in Sylva. Sylva was where the largest population of African American lived. The other outlying communities complied with the consolidation. These areas were Webster, Hog Rock, Dillsboro, River View, and the Sylva area.

For three years, Cullowhee refused to allow their children to be

bused to Sylva. With Cullowhee without a teacher, the school was closed and the School Committee wanted the county to allow them to build another one-room school in the Montieth Gap. They wanted the building to be next to Mt. Carmel Baptist Church. Lumber was already stacked up near the church, but the school was never built. Consolidation with African American school in Sylva was the plan to defray the cost of education for the African American students. Instead of paying for four one-room   schools, the students were bused to Sylva.

In 1925, the Cullowhee area children were bused to Sylva. It was the beginning of bussing in Jackson County. Estus returned to school, only to dropout when his father needed him. With the school a year longer, Estus was determined to finish the eighth grade. He could read, count money, and write his name. These three educational tools were important to Papa George. When Estus received his diploma on April 21, 1928, he never returned to school, at least not to the hallow halls. As he went through life, he learned from the world around him.

My father, Mr. George Estus Casey was a jack-of –all trade and master at all of them. When he married Miss DeRosette Horne from Asheville, he bought land from Aunt Mell Chavis and built a house for his growing family. His wife gave him the plan and he erected it. At first it was a single level house that was built high off the ground.

When his family grew, he closed in the basement; converting the house into a two-story structure. He built three sets of bunk beds that allowed all the nine children to have a bed of their own. Upstairs there were four bed rooms and a huge living room with a small area for a piano and built-in bookcases. Downstairs was a playroom, dining room, kitchen, bathroom, which had a sink and large galvanized tub installed as a bath tub and a wash room with a packed dirt floor.

My father obtained most of the materials from Western Carolina Teachers College where he worked as a cook for about eight years. His boss hassled him continuously. They had an argument and my father walked away and never went back, although Western tried to get him to return. After that my father had several jobs. He was a servant, carpenter, cook, and farrier. But most important, he received his grammar grade diploma.

This is just one story about an African American boy who had a desire to get an education.

Bussing in Jackson County

Cullowhee/Old Cullowhee Road/Ashe Settlement
Dillsboro/Sylva/Tannery Flats/Scotts Creek

B ussing a child out of its district to have balance of black and white in a school caused a tremendous amount of problems during the 1960s. As early as 1924, Jackson County sent its black students to central school in Sylva. The school bus ride to the colored school in Jackson County, North Carolina was long and tiresome.

The worse part about it was the half-mile walk to the bus line to board the old number 18. Wintertime always presented a problem as the Estus Casey children waited for the bus to arrive to take them on the long trek to Central Consolidated School in Sylva, which was out of the school district for Cullowhee Valley students. However, this was the time of segregation when black and white students could not attend the same school. Most of the white students walked a country mile to their school.

Bundled up in winter clothing, which included a wool sweater under the outer thick coat and gloves to warm the cold aching hands, each child walked slowly to the bus line. There were thick socks on their feet and the new shoes they had gotten just before school opened in September. For the girls these were the hard thick eraser red rubber soles of their black and white oxfords; while the three boys wore brown brogans under their long johns and jeans. Sadly, for the girls, there were not any long trousers to stop the cold winter wind from shooting up the coconut-butter shiny-brown, skinny legs.

In essence, it was cold on this early November morning in 1952! Now the Casey children had reached their bus stop, which was only a few feet from the main highway in "downtown" Cullowhee. All the noise and the smells of the morning filled the air. The pungent smell of gasoline lingered as cars passed on their way to work at the college or the laboratory school that was under the auspice of the Jackson County School system.

Perhaps the odor originated from Watson's Sawmill that operated on the lower river road where the Casey children passed each day on their sojourn to catch the bus. In fact, this part of the dusty country road was covered with sawdust and lined with stacks of lumber that sometimes allowed them to use their imagination.

"That pile of lumber looks like a skyscraper I saw in a magazine at school."

"I guess you could say that."

"Just look how tall it is."

The little ones stretched their necks and looked at the high stacks of lumber. The distorted look from their angle indeed gave credence to that perception. Engaging in conservation always seemed to take one's mind off the cold morning air. Even the sound of the huge blade saw humming along at the sawmill could be turned into music. Although, they no longer observed this operation, their minds remembered the chips flying as the saw rendered the log into a smooth piece of lumber.

A service station helped the smells and the sounds of morning. It was situated on the same road where the children stood. With innocence eyes, they espied the activities that took place there. Gas was being pumped. Tires were being changed. Hoods of car were being opened as the attendant's head disappeared from view. These things took their minds off the coldness that penetrated their clothes.

Waiting for the bus to come always seemed like an eternity. Therefore, they watched the white folks. It was fascinating to behold the white students who walked up the road. In their arms were books and notebooks. They wore store bought clothes and their girls' hair-dos were perfect if they did not have it wrapped in a fancy headscarf.

"Where are they going?" One of the little ones inquired, "Where are they going?"

"School."

"School?"

'Where?"

"Just up the road."

"They walk."

"Why can't we just go to school up there?"

"You can't. It ain't for colored folks."

At that moment, the bus went up the road. Everything about the white school was lost as they prepared themselves for the long ride to the colored school. Patiently they waited for the bus to go to Long Branch, which was beyond the college, to pick up a student. After leaving Long Branch and driving through the college campus, which housed the white high school in the McKee Building, the bus turned to the right at the college entrance and head to Mt. Zion AME Zion Methodist Church's parking lot. There he picked up the students who waited there before rolling to a stop at the Casey children.

The screeching sound of the brakes and the welcome opening of the bus's double door, signaled the Casey children to step up and board the bus. Although the bus was practically empty, each child scrambled to find "their" seat. The little ones sat on the horse, which were two long low benches back to back in the middle of the bus. The older children selected window seats, which faced the front. An adult passenger was on the bus for it was permitted for them to hitch a ride to Sylva, which was the hub of activity for the county since it be-came the county seat in the early 1900's.

Slowly the bus started up again and made its way across the Tuckaseigee Bridge that connected Cullowhee to the rest of the county. They rebuilt the bridge after the 1940 flood destroyed the original structure and the little valley of Cullowhee put on a new face. Gone were all the structures of the 19th century with the 20th century all around them.

Navigating the curvey paved road, the bus and its passengers crawled slovenly out of the Cullowhee school district. On the way to its destination, the school bus passed through two school districts,

Dillsboro and Webster to end up in the Sylva school district where the colored students were bussed. It was all because the General Assembly passed a bill that colored children could not be taught by a white teacher and vice versa.

The bus's first stop after the Casey children boarded, was on the way to Sylva. On the Old Cullowhee Road after a sharp curve, the bus stopped and waited for a student who used a cable stung across the river guide him as he poled himself across. These colored folks lived on the other side of the river in Montieth Gap, which was still in the Cullowhee school district. In fairness, they could have walked to school as the white students did.

Now the bus chugged on to the next stop, which was in a straight-away with a sharp deep curve in front of it. Again, students had to be poled across the river. Mr. Will Rogers navigated the boat across with his young children and grandchildren to catch the bus. Around the curve, the Claude Young children came on board. Now it was on to the driver's house. Professor Frank parked the bus, got out and went into his home. After eating breakfast, he emerged with his two children in toll. That was the last stop in the Cullowhee district.

After rounding another curve, the bus made a left turn, going over Ashe Settlement Bridge to enter into the Webster school district. The bus bounced along the unpaved dirt road. At the top of the hill, which was the entry to Hog Rock, the bus turned right and headed to a little white church where the Bryson and the Allen boys waited on the bus. The bus turned around and back toward the bridge as it turned left coming out of Hog Rock.

If the bus had turned the right and continued down the road, they would have viewed Webster school situated on a hill welcoming the white students. However, the colored children who lived in little coves like Hog Rock, Webster and Little Savannah could not attend.

Leaving the Ashe Settlement behind, the bus again crossed the bridge and made a left turn to Sylva. On the way, they passed the Rolling Green Community that led up to Locust Creek where Professor Frank spent his childhood.

The bus traveled to downtown Sylva where the adult passenger Mr. A. B. Burkes got off.

"If you need a ride home," Professor Frank said, "I'll pick you up around here around three."

"Thanks, 'Fessor Frank. I'll hitch a ride before that."

Mr. Burkes threw up his hand in a salutation and started toward back street. When the bus door closed, the journey continued out of town on into the little hamlet of Dillsboro and its subdivision of River View. Because of the railroad, Dillsboro had become a busy hub of activities, thereby an influx of colored folks had settled. The Jarrett House was the only hotel, but blacks obtained jobs as chambermaids, washerwomen, handymen, and cooks.

Some African Americans settled in downtown Dillsboro, while others found large tracts of land along the Tuckaseigee River. These mountainous terraces sometimes made it difficult to make a living. Nevertheless, they did not give up, because it was a safe haven for them. In this subdivision, they built their homes and erected a Baptist church with a one-room school in the community, which they called River View. When the county ordered the consolidation of all the colored one-room schools, River View complied.

Now on this cold November morning, number 18 made its appearance in Dillsboro. Just as the scene in Cullowhee, white children walked to their district school that was located across the railroad track in a little cove. From the bus window, the children saw the building, as the bus chugged across the tracks to venture into the unpaved road of River View. Balls of dust and steam from the bus trailed the yellow vehicle as it made its journey to the turnaround spot on River View road. Destination was the River View Baptist Church parking lot.

As the bus made its way to the turnaround spot, Professor Frank always slowed down when he approached a white student walking toward his school. Out of courtsey, he waved at him, as did the students on the bus. Looking back at the student, he seemed to be staring almost in anger at the bus. Slowly, he turned and continued his mile walk to school.

When the bus got to the turn spot designated by county, there were colored students waiting to board the bus. How many boarded the bus depended on the extended families who moved in over the summer. There were the Pettit's, the Arnolds, the Mingus's, the Whittenburgs, the Gaithers and the Howells. Several students boarded the bus and by springtime, some would be gone.

There would be one more stop on the trip down the dusty road. Their compound was the first colored home in River View set stately on a hill overlooking the Tuckaseigee River. Just to view the white freshly painted house from down the long set of steps was gorgeous and elegant. It shouted out to the other colored folks home that they had made it. In the back of their home was a fruit orchard that yielded an income for the Wells.

As the bus stopped in front of the steps and Professor Frank honked the horn, two children raced out of the house to catch the bus. While waiting for them to navigate the steps, a couple of white students hurried by. Their turned-up faces looked not too happy about walking to school.

When the bus got to "downtown" Dillsboro, it stopped in front of the Jarrett House and picked up a student. Other students were picked up at the edge of the hamlet, before heading back to Sylva. The bus stopped at the entrance of town at the fountain just below the courthouse. African American kids gathered there from the little coves in and around the courthouse. They walked to the fountain from Freeze Hill and Watson Cove to get to school, which was just about one and half mile away.

The last stop was in the heart of the African American community in the county called Tannery Flats. The bus's seating accommodation was only half-full until the colored students in Tannery Flats boarded the bus. It was only recently that these students rode the bus for they were just one mile from school. It was the county's policy for any student who lived within a mile of the school to walk.

Therefore, in the beginning of the consolidation of the one-room colored schools, the students in the Flats walked the creek bank to get to school. Sometimes when the bus was late, some of the children would walk to school.

Whence this long bus ride out of the district for most the colored students meant that they rode a bus, while some of the white students walked the mile to their district school. These white students could not understand why African American students waved at them from a bus while they walked. At least, the white student went to the school in his own district, which was just a country mile away.

Virginia Bennett and Ann Rogers rode the bus from Cullowhee to Sylva.

The Colored Men of the Tannery
Tannery Flats

T he Tannery whistle blew; everyone knew it was time to be at work or time to go home. Perhaps it was lunchtime. No matter, the colored men of the Tannery woke up, worked, and ate by the sound of the whistle. It was a good sound on Saturday when they finished a week's work. Now it was time to become a human again, to relax, to be with family, or perhaps find some entertainment.

It wass the early 1900's when the Harris-Reese Tannery started its operation. Northern born C. J. Harris came to Jackson County to

 find a fortune after the Civil War. Local white businessmen, David Hall and E. L. McKee partnered with Harris in some of his ventures. One of those was the Sylva Supply Co where the tannery worker redeemed their coupons to buy supplies for the week. When payday came, Sylva Supply got their money from the coupons a worker bought. Now the worker was back in debt again because sometimes he only got about a dollar or less. Therefore, this colored tannery worker owed his soul to the company store.

Most of these colored tannery workers arrived in Sylva from other places in the county. They came from Beta, Hog Rock, and Old Settlement to find work in the Tannery. They heard they were hiring both black and white workers. For most blacks, farming was difficult because the land they owned was too rocky or just mountains. It was no good for farming.

They came to Sylva and settled in the community close to the

Tannery. Instead of having to travel a country mile to work, most of them just walked. Harris and his partners set up company houses for those who worked at the Tannery. Dotted across the hill of Tannery Flats were red company houses for the worker and his family to occupy. Therefore, they came with their meager belongings to work and get a regular paycheck. They worked 10-hour days for $1.10 a day.

By the 1900's the black population reached almost 400. With Harris Enterprises, there was work for all. Some of these early workers were Mr. Josh Worley, Mr. Grant Wilson, Mr. Joe Love, Mr. Tom Pickens, Mr. Lester McDonald, Mr. John Austin, Mr. Bob Bryson, Mr. Homer Whittenburg, Mr. Clarence Love, and Mr. McKinley Whittenburg. They worked there around 1918. Some remained there until it finally closed in 1957.

Working in the tannery was hard and a filthy job. When the hides arrived, they rolled about twenty of them on huge wheels. They tied the shanks together and rolled them to soak in lime. After that, they took it to be soaked in water, then back to the lime line. This was to make sure all the flesh was off the hides. It took weeks to accomplish this.

Then the hides went to the beam shock and on to an unhairing machine. The workers dried them again. It seemed that they recycled the hides by soaking the hair for a few minutes then drying it and shipping out.

In the meanwhile, they placed the hides in a machine that removed the remaining flesh. When this flesh came off, they put the

hides in a huge vat to be cooked. The company sold grease and tal-
low. After the hides went through this process, workers took an especially made large instrument, which had a blade on one edge and a
saw on the other. This tedious job removed the remaining flesh. The
workers placed them in vat, where they remained for a couple of days.

Afterward they put them in a tanning processing vat for several
days. A worker moved the hides to vats outside and a worker took
them out. They stacked up the hides on flat boards until there were
tons of them. Then they took them to the leather cropper where they
cut off the bellies. After that, the skins were sent back though the tanning process for an additional week or so.

Some of the workers continued to work with the hides until a re-
fine piece of leather resulted that could be make into shoes and other
things. This process took about nine months before they shipped it
out to their customers. In meanwhile, the process started all over
again with a new load of hides.

This was when they only processed hides. They also began to
process bark. At first, the company only used chestnut bark. As time
went on, they accepted other tree bark.

In 1928, the Sylva Paperboard Company opened. However, it did
not hire black workers. Separation of the work force in Jackson
County caught up with the rest of the country. Lyndon McKee, who
was the manager of Armour Tannery, sold his chestnut chip byproduct
to George H. Mead. Then he arranged for Mead to buy Armour's ex-
tract operation and to establish the paperboard company, which later
became Mead Corporation. Mead became the largest manufacturing
company in the county. It employed 300 workers, which were white
until the 1960's.

Therefore, the black man had to look elsewhere to find work. At
the Tannery, there was no pension plan. Thirty years of struggling to
make a buck was over. Most of the colored tannery workers uprooted
their families and headed north before the closing of the tannery in
1957. Some would come back to visit, while others did not.

The Songbird of the Tannery Flats: Miss Gertie
Black Branch/Tannery Flats

U p above their heads, they heard music in the air. It was the melodious voice of Mrs. Gertrude Amanda Gaither McDowell as she went about household chores. Mrs. Gertrude was born on July 1, 1892 in the Sylva Township. She died in on November 11, 1971. Her mother and father's names were lost in history. However, her father's last name was Gaither. In 1911, she married Mr. Walter Fred McDowell, who migrated to Tannery Flats with his parents from the Webster area.

His parents were Mr. Allen McDowell and Mrs. Rachel Robinson McDowell. Mr. McDowell was born in McDowell County and Rachel was from South Carolina. They came to the Webster area around the late 1800's and settled in the Black Branch community of Hog Rock. Since Webster was the county seat, it would be excellent place to find employment.

Therefore the small black community built a Methodist church, which they named Black Branch Methodist Church. At this time the mica mines were not hiring anymore and farming the land was becoming too difficult to support a family.

By the 1900's, the McDowell's decided to move again. It seemed that Sylva Tanning Company was hiring both black and white workers. Allen felt that it would be a good economical move, but spiritually they were hesitant. The Tannery Flats area did not have a Methodist church, but Liberty Baptist was just up the road. He promised his wife that they would build one in the heart of the community.

They moved to Tannery Flats and he obtained a job in the Tannery. Their son, Walter came with them and found work there, too. He also found his soul mate, Miss Gertrude Amanda McDowell. Everyone called her Gertie and that is the name which appeared on the couple's marriage certificate. Religiously, they were a mixed couple. Walter was a Methodist and Miss Gertie was a Baptist.

It seemed that Allen and Rachel, along with other former members of Black Branch Methodist Church partitioned the African Methodist Episcopal Zion Church Organization to help them to acquire small lot in the Flats to build a church. On March 24, 1910,

AMEZ purchased a lot from J. R. Love and Ida E. Love.

By 1914, a small framed white plank building was erected in the heart of the Flats. In honor of their presiding elder George Maize, they named their church Maize Chapel AME Zion. Allen had kept his promise to his wife, Rachel. A Methodist Church sat right in the middle of the black community in the Tannery Flats.

Miss Gertie joined and became an active member. She loved to sing, especially the old Negro spirituals. With her family which would include three children by 1923, she spend most her time at home attending her children, Genetra, Warren Theodore, and Robert Lee.

The McDowell house set upon the bank on the upper road of the Flats. Every Wednesday, she would be outside doing the weekly wash. She used a washboard and a tub to wash. As she scrubbed the clothes up and down the washboard, she would sing. Her beautiful

voice echoed throughout the community.

Just beyond the railroad tracks, the Sylva Tannery was located. As Walter worked he could hear his wife's melodious voice above the machinery that hummed its own tune. Some-

times, he would pause for a moment, and then he would go back to work. However it was always a gospel tune coming from his lips.

Her voice seemed to mesmerize the other workers and the loggers from Pine Creek with their load of tanning bark. As they entered the yard of the Tannery to unload their wagons of strips of bark, the men heard her singing. Pulling up the wagons driven by oxen, the men paused to listen.

One of the old Negro spirituals "Swing Low, Sweet Chariot" was heard, as Miss Gertie washed her clothes and the men at the Tannery unloaded the strip bark. Before they left Miss Gertie sang another song. Her washing was done and she began to hang them on the line. The loggers placed the strip bark on the ground for the Tannery workers to gather up the bundle and take it to be processed. When the loggers left, Miss Gertie's voice rang in their ears as she sang "Lay Down my Burden."

Miss Gertie lived to be seventy-nine years old. She outlived her husband, Walter who died of cirrhosis of the liver in 1941 and her oldest son Warren who died from two gunshot wounds in 1953.

However, she continued to sing praise to the Lord. A faithful member of her adopted church, she attended the regular services as well as the Feast in the Wilderness. A tall soft-spoken lady, Miss Gertie sang like a caged bird until she died.

Molly Worley and Alice Turk Mingus: Midwives
Webster/River View/Tannery Flats

There is little known about Molly Worley and Alice Turk Mingus. However, both were midwives, who served the black and white communities during the 1920's and 1930's. From the Register of Deeds office, there is some data about Alice Turk Mingus. However, time has erased the existence of Molly Worley. To Ben Coleman Fisher, she was his family washerwoman who lived in Websster. Twice a week, she came to fetch and return laundry.

However, she was more than a washerwoman. She was also a midwife to the black community when the doctor was not available. Looking through the birth records at the Register of Deeds; her name was listed on some registered birth certificates as the midwife.

Although, she is listed as a midwife, there is no record of her death. Fisher vividly recalled that she was a tall black African woman. She had beautiful white teeth, gold earrings and a marvelous smile. On her head, she carried a large, square, hickory-splint basket, which was full of clean or dirty laundry. The most fascinating thing about her carrying the basket was that she balanced it on her head without touching it with her hands.

She crossed through the cow pasture fences, which had few gates. However, there were plenty of stiles, which went to the top of the fence. At the top was a small platform that was only about two feet wide. Molly came through the pasture lane and walked up the steps on one side of stiles. Then she did a little jig on the platform and hopped down the steps to the other side. While performing this with white children followong her, she had the basket of laundry on her head. She never dropped the basket, nor did it appear as if it was going to fall off.

More than being a washerwoman, she had a storehouse of witch and haunt stories. She told these African tales to her customer's children. If it was late in the day when Molly arrived and left, those ghostly tales remained fresh in those children's mind. When bedtime came, they were afraid to go their bedroom alone.

The African ghost stories are lost, just as the art of keeping a basket on your head. Like most African American culture in the mountains of Western North Carolina, these arts have been assimilated into Appalachian culture.

****

In the history of Dillsboro, Minnie Dills Gray reduced the importance of the colored pioneers to the last page of Dillsboro's history. She produced three photographs of these African American pioneers which included Alice Turk and her mother Mrs. Nancy Turk, who served Wesley Enloe' family during the last part of the Civil War. According to this Dillsboro history, W. A. Enloe did not come to the area until after the Civil War. However, Aunt Nancy (as the whites called Alice's mother) was a black respected women who remained in the Enloe household until about 1908. W. A. Enloe was a merchant who operated two stores in downtown Dillsboro. Therefore it is speculated that Mrs. Nancy was a paid servant in the Enloe household.

On January 17, 1877, Alice was born in the Webster Township to Mr. Clark and Nancy Howell Turk. Her father Clark came over the hill from South Carolina and her mother Nancy was from Swain County, North Carolina. She was educated in the segregated school system in Jackson County in the one-room black school in the Webster Township. Besides working in the white man's kitchen, she became a midwife. Her death certificate recorded at Jackson County's Register of Deed verified that she was a midwife. Alice delivered both black and white babies in the Sylva and Dillsboro area.

When she was on her way to deliver a baby, she carried a little black bag. As she walked through the neighborhood, the children knew that someone was going to have a new brother or a new sister. The children would stop and stare at her black bag, because they thought that the baby was in it.

She was married to Shannon Mingus and made their home in Dillsboro. The Mingus, like most black lived in the River View area around the River View Baptist Church. At the time of her death in 1939, she was sixty-two years old. Mrs. Alice Turk Mingus was buried in River View on March 22, 1939.

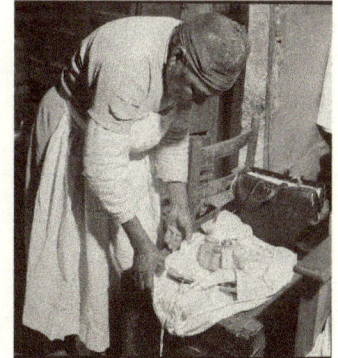

Mr. Silas Davis: Boarding House Operator
Sile Davis Ford

At River Bend Road between Cullowhee and Sylva, Silas Davis ran a boarding house. In the late 1800's and the early 1900's when Jackson County's transportation system was not fully developed, Silas Davis provided an alternative to the problem. The Tuckaseigee River meandered its way to Sylva. However, at some places, it was too shallow to transport supplies from Cullowhee area to Sylva. Industries were beginning to develop because the Tannery and other lumber related businesses.

For the men at Pine Creek, it was imperative that they get their load of tanning bark to the Tannery in Sylva. Wagons loaded with the strips of bark were difficult to travel over the steep grade of Montieth Gap to get to the Sile Davis Ford. Most would cross the river in Cullowhee and take the road to Sylva. However, on their return trip home, they chose to go by the way of Sile Davis Ford. Their empty wagons pulled by oxen could make the trek easily.

When the shadows of the day came, they stopped and spent the night at Sile Davis Ford. Besides fording the river there, a campground just at the riverside welcomed them. If they wanted to bed down in a more comfortable setting, they stayed at Silas's house, which set on about fifty or more acres of land. The house was a two-story framed building that once housed his family. Now he and his wife lived alone and strangers were welcome to abode in the upstairs bedrooms.

Morning always brought the smell of breakfast cooking in the Davis house. After breakfast, the boarders departed and the Davises went about their daily chores. Travelers, whether walking or riding, could cut about mile off their journey home.

Silas Davis

home place was the east side of the river and Montieth Gap was on the west of the river.

Who was Silas Davis? He was a former slave born in April of 1827 to a slave of David Rogers in Cullowhee. In 1854, he was sold to Isaac Davis, a Native American. The 1860 Census of Jackson County listed Isaac Davis as a head of a household. There were five people in his household. His personal and real estates were worth about $2200 dollars. However, on the Slave Schedule, Isaac was not among the slaveholders.

It seemed that Silas Davis married a girl named Sarah. Four children are born to this union. They were Thomas (1851-1913), Wade (1856), Hattie (1858) and Robert (1861). Mr. Davis probably built the two-story house for his family. In 1876, he claimed a 50 (more or less) tract of land. By the time he claimed the land, his children were grown. Robert was 15, Hattie was 18, Wade was 20 and Thomas was 29.

The death of Sarah, Silas's first wife, is unknown. However, on January 18, 1880, when Silas Davis was 52 years old, he married Susan Sherrill, who was also 52 years old. They married at Silas' house with Justice of the Peace R. G. Watson conducting the ceremony. As witnesses to the nuptial, D. H. Phillips and J.D. Moore signed the marriage certificate.

Together, Silas and Susan ran the boarding house, as wagons, horses and walkers came across Sile Davis Ford. These boarders stayed overnight because it took more than a day's journey to get home. Perhaps some were strangers just seeking shelter for the night.

Deacon Emory E. Curry: Plumber
Freeze Hill, Scott Creek

Mr. Emory M. Curry came to the Sylva area in the early 1900's. According to 1900 Federal Census taken on June 2 in Georgia, Emory was 18 years old and living with his widowed mother, Mrs. Catherine Bruce Curry, who was the head of the household. Living also in the home were four other children. They were Logan, who was 15 years old, Grady, who was 11 years old, Fannie, who was eight, and Sam, who was only one year old. Her husband was Mr. Sam Curry, perhaps died shortly before their son Sam was born. The family was living in Franklin, Georgia in the Bryant District. Mrs. Curry listed her occupation as a day laborer, but had been unable to find work. She and her children lived on a farm. Like his mother, Emory was also a day laborer.

Mrs. Curry was born in 1866, just shortly after the Civil War. Both her parents Mr. Wesley Hooper and Mrs. Rebecca Williams Hooper were born in Hart County, Georgia, which suggest they were former slaves in the Bryant District of Lavonia County, which is located northeast of Atlanta about an hour and a half drive away. The county is situated on the coast of Georgia. Whether the Curry's' and their people were slaves is not known. Catherine and her children could read and write.

When Mr. Emory Curry arrived in Sylva, North Carolina, he was a married man and brought his family with him. He was married to Clarina (Clarence) and the couple had a son. On the 1930 Federal Census, he listed his occupation as a plumber. In the household were his wife Clarina and their son Ben who was born in 1914 in Georgia.

Mr. Emory Curry and his family came to Jackson County sometimes between 1920 and 1925. They joined Liberty Baptist Church and he became a deacon in 1925 while Rev. W. M. Hamilton was the pastor. Becoming a deacon in the largest African American church in the county gave Emory more status in the African American community.

Being a skilled plumber, Emory served his community of Freeze Hill, as well as African Americans in the Tannery Flats. He established himself and did work for the Appalachian whites as well as the African Americans. Being known as an honest man among the Appalachian whites, he was respected in the larger society.

His wife died in 1932, at 34 years of age. Through the church, he met the recently divorced Mamie Wilson Hyatt. After a short courtship, they married. She was about 25 years old and Mr. Emory Curry was almost 50 years old. This was a good move for Deacon Curry to be married to native girl from a good family.

Now he had two additions to his family. Mamie had a daughter from her previous marriage, Dorothy Hyatt. Together, they became a family. When Ben became a young adult, he left Sylva, but Dorothy remained in Sylva and married Sylvester Love.

Freeze Hill was in the middle of town, but Mr. Emory moved to the Scotts Creek area where Liberty Baptist and Central Consolidated were located. He built a house just below the preacher's house. Therefore, he was involved with the African American school committee. In 1948, Central Consolidated School decided to organize a PTA and to join the North Carolina Congress of Colored Parents and Teachers, Inc. He served as vice president and was on PTA's City Service Committee. One of their duties was to assist in the nationwide effort to provide qualified teachers for the school. This gave him a chance to interact with the Appalachian white society.

It is said that Mr. Curry loved children. A tall heavy man, he laughed and played with children in the neighborhood. Therefore, it was natural for him to have an interest in their welfare.

When the Board of Education decided to build a new brick school for the African Americans, Mr. Curry was called in to see and approve the plans of the new structure. This was shortly before Brown vs. Topeka went before the Supreme Court and declared that separate educational facilities were not equal. Integration was just around the corner and the plans were tabled. However, Raleigh gave the school superintendent, Vernon Cope, to go on with the plans.

Mr. Emory Curry was there, along with other African American leaders, to approve of the school plans. The plans had been modified, but the African American leaders, who had no children in the all-African American school, approved them.

On August 30, 1956 Mr. Emory Curry passed away. It was just days away from the opening of the new school, Jackson School for the African American students which would include his grandsons, William, Joe and Tommy Love.

Wilsy Dorsey: A Field of Dreams
Tannery Flats

Baseball became the sport most blacks played long before Jackie Robinson became the first black to participate in the Major Leagues. Showing off their skills on a field of dreams, most black boys played the game. Just by taking a stick and tossing a rock in the air, youngsters played baseball by themselves. With the roar of the "crowd" in his ears, he would attempt to hit the rock and send it flying through the air. It all came down to skill and timing.

It appeared that Wilsy Dorsey had both--skill and timing. Around the Tannery Flats, he was halted an excellent baseball player. He could hit the ball a country mile and was an excellent pitcher. In other words, Mr. Wilsy Dorsey was a superb baseball player. Therefore, it became a challenge to the other black players to outdo him.

Wilsy Dorsey was the son of Mr. Solomon and Mrs. Mintie Oats Dorsey. His father, from Tennessee, met his mother in the little hamlet of Dillsboro. Wilsy's (sometimes spelled Wilse) given name was Wilson. He was born on June 8, 1900. He went to the segregated one-room school in Jackson County and finished his school at Cherryville High School or Lincoln Academy.

When he finished his schooling, he went to work for Armour Tanning Company. He married Gladys Enloe from Dillsboro. From this marriage, there were eight children. There were five girls and three boys. The girls were Mildred (1919), Taretho (1926), Lucy Ann (1928), Barbara Gene (1930), and Joe Nell (1933). Their sons were

Paul Abraham (1921), David (1923) and Preston (1936).

From childhood, Wilsy played baseball with relative and friends. In high school, he played on the baseball team. As a young man, he continued to play the game with bets on the sides. They laid out a baseball field adjacent to the Tannery in the Tannery Flats. Like Wilsy, most of the players were Tannery workers. Sunday afternoon was time to play a game. Each Fourth of July celebration, they played baseball. Whites and blacks came to see Wilsy play.

When World War I was raging overseas, Wilsy was on the baseball diamond. A lad of 17, he played with an integrated team. It was a semi-pro team, which played games all over the South. Taretho (Tracy Butler), his daughter, related to me that Wilsy was known as an excellent pitcher. His oldest daughter, Mrs. Mildred Dorsey Conley told me that he was a great baseball player and the best in Jackson County.

There is no record of his feats in the game of baseball, but those who are alive can remember Mr. Wilsy Dorsey. As an old-timer said, "He could hit that ball a country mile as well as throw a mean curve ball.

Unfortunately for Wilsy life did not give him an equal playing field. With his growing family and his desire to play professional baseball, he turned to liquor to bury his dreams. An alcoholic, Wilsy died at the prime of his life. On October 29, 1940, he passed away from chronic alcoholism and cancer of the stomach and liver. That was seven years too early for Wilsy. In 1947, Jackie Robinson became the first black player in the modern major league baseball history (although in 1884 the American Association major league club known as the Toledo Mudhens had two blacks on their roster).

Wilsy's grandson, Herbert Conley, son of Mr. Alvin Conley and Mrs. Mildred Dorsey Conley was an excellent athlete. He played baseball with an organized all-black club in Sylva. He pitched for the Sylva Red Sox. While in high school at segregated Jackson School, he played basketball. The apple does not fall too far from the tree.

The Church Organist: Miss Ethel May Fisher
Webster/ Freeze Hill

Miss Ethel May Fisher was born on January 6, 1900 to Della Brown and Eldis Fisher in the Webster Township. She attended the Black Webster one-room school. By the time of consolidation for all the black one-room schools in the county, she was a young lady of 21. By then, she joined the work force of the county by becoming a domestic servant to well-off white folks in and around Webster.

With her parents, she attended the Black Webster Baptist Church and became a member at an early age. Miss Ethel loved to sing and play the church organ, which she taught herself. She played mostly by ear. Although her home church did not have an organ, she played the one at River View Baptist when the churches came together for Feast in the Wilderness.

Ethel married Mr. Elsie Blakely, whose folks came to the mountain from just over the hill in Clayton, Georgia. They had four daughters, Katherine, Betty, Barbara Ann, and Shirley and three sons, Clifford, Wilson, and Elsie Jr. She taught her daughters how to play the organ and piano.

While in Webster, she worked for the Montieth family. In the fall issue of the 1983 Historic Webster, Janice Montieth Blanton recalled that Mrs. Blakely worked for her family. She stated that Ethel was jolly and loved to talk. Although she was an excellent worker, she loved to play and talk to the Montieth children. Therefore, their mother tried to steer the children away.

Sometimes it did not work. The children loved to talk to her and found ways to escape their mother's watchful eye. When Ethel cleaned the children's room, the children followed her. Janice recalled that they flopped on the bed face-down and begged Ethel to tickle them. She started "walking her fingers" at their feet and slowly moved up their backs. When they could no longer stand Ethel's "walking fingers," they laughed hysterically. Mrs. Montieth heard them and sent them outside so Ethel could work.

When Ethel received her pay from Mrs. Montieth, she wrapped the money in a handkerchief. After carefully tying it up, she swiftly put it in her bra between her breasts. She never took anything from the Montieth household without permission. If she found any loose change, while cleaning, she gave it to Mrs. Montieth.

When Mr. Blakely died, she bought a house on Freeze Hill in Sylva. Her children went to the segregated consolidated school in the Scotts Creek area in Sylva. Being in Sylva, she obtained another housekeeping job in Dillsboro at the Cannons. After working for the Montieth, she worked mainly for the Cannons. She cleaned house and took care of their children. As always, the pay was not much, but it kept body and soul together.

Miss Ethel always had a smile on her face. She could joke with the best of them. Working in a household full of children's laugher, I am sure Mrs. Ethel Blakely contributed to their laughter. Her "walking fingers" tiptoed across their back and tickled the ivory on piano or organ.

Praising God was important to her. She always tried to find her way to church each Sunday, singing, playing the piano and praising God's name. This gift she gave to her children and grandchildren.

The Perfect Couple: Mr. Ode and Miss Hattie Bryson
Tannery Flats

For seventy-seven years, Mr. Ode Fred Bryson and Mrs. Hattie Howell Bryson enjoyed matrimonial bliss. There were some good times, as well as bad times. However, the good times seemed to outweigh the bad. They were the prefect couple, because not only did they love each other, but also they each brought some-thing to their marriage--marriage based on mutual trust.

Mr. Ode Fred was born to George Hill and Della Shepard on Au-gust 1, 1897. It was apparent that the young couple was not married. Miss Shepard gave the child up and Ode grew up in the home of a Bryson. Naturally, he took Bryson as his last name and retained that last name for the rest of his life.

Unfortunately for Ode, he did not get much book learning. As a result he could not read or write. Work was the primary concern of most black families. Therefore, book learning was not the top of the list in importance. However, it was imperative to know your numbers and to know the monetary value of money. Just to recognize the value of the different legal tender, which included coins as well as the greenbacks, was essential to his existence.

As Ode grew up, he learned the trade of a mason. He helped build walls, fireplaces and other rock structures. However, before he became a master of his trade, he worked at the tannery. When Mead Corporation established itself in the Tannery Flats, he helped build their smoke stack around 1920's. Mr. Ode said that he laid the first brick.

In 1974, Mead closed and Dixie Paper bought the plant. About ten years later, they tore down the old smoke stacks. As Mr. Ode watched, tears came to his eyes as he remembered being the first worker to lay bricks for the foundation. For him, they destroyed part of his history and visual testimony of his work. From his home on the hill on Allen Street, he could see the smoke stacks. Now they were gone from the skyline.

Nevertheless, Mr. Ode and Mrs. Hattie had each other, their chil-dren, grandchildren and greats of which to be proud. A prefect couple who raised eight children, perhaps met around 1912 at Liberty Baptist Church. Perhaps they knew each other most of their life. The couple had been a member of Liberty Baptist for almost eighty years or more. Mrs. Hattie was active in the church. She was a member of the Y.M.A. Missionary and the Usher Board.

Yet what make this couple perfect? Remaining together for seventy-seven years is a plus, as they grew old together. They were able to own their home, which set on the hill on Allen Street in the Tannery Flats. With Mr. Ode not being able to read, he chose a partner for life who could read and write.

Miss Hattie Howell was born December 16, 1896 in the River View Community. She was the daughter of Mr. Lee Howell and Mrs. Laura Dorsey Howell. Growing up in River View, she obtained her schooling at the one-room black school in the area. She joined Liberty Baptist at an early age and remained a member until she died June 30, 1991.

Although Miss Hattie could read, she had difficult adding numbers. When she got married, she relied on Mr. Ode to deal with the finances. She would raise their children, cook and clean, maintaining a nice home for Mr. Ode.

Mr. Ode and Miss Hattie tied the knot in 1914. She was 15 years old and Ode was 17. From that union, eight children were born. There were five boys and three girls. The boys were James, Bob, George, Hal and Daniel. The girls were Laura, Martha Jean and Anna Liz. When the PTA organized in 1948, Mrs. Hattie joined. She served as a Grade Mother for the high school department. Mr. Ode was also involved with the education of their children.

Most of time, when one saw Mr. Ode, Miss Hattie was not far away. The couple went together. Beginning in 1982, Jackson County's VOICE program helped the couple. A volunteer took them each Friday to the grocery store, to doctor's appointments and to pay their debts. In 1988, they attended 'Celebrate 90' at the Golden Age Club. At that time, Miss Hattie was 90 and Ode was 93. The couple enjoyed events for the senior citizens until Miss Hattie died. At the age of 98, Mr. Ode joined his mate on March 30, 1996.

Uncle Charlie Casey: Charity Begins at Home
Peter's Bluff

Uncle Charlie Casey, known for his generosity, was the baby boy of Bill and Amanda Thomas Casey. He was born April 2, 1884 at home in the Qualla area. His family moved to the Cullowhee/Webster area in about 1892 when his parents bought areas of mountainous land from M. L. Deitz and his wife D. J. Deitz for $300 dollars. Educated in the segregated school system in Jackson County, he went to the one-room black school on Thomas Davis Hill in Cullowhee.

He married Hattie Emley Davis, the daughter of Mr. Thomas and Mrs. Lena Davis. They moved from the old homestead and built their home on land Aunt Hattie inherited from her father. From that marriage, they had five children. Twins, a boy and girl, were stillbirths in 1918. Their next child, Maud was born in 1919. William was born two years later with a daughter May Mary Anne Ruth made her appearance in 1922.

With the family complete, tragedy occurred on July 23, 1924. Five years old Maud died from a burn received from a hearth fire. Apparently, she got too close to the fire while Aunt Hattie was cooking or washing clothes and her clothing ignited into flames. Being a child, she probably ran, which fanned the flames. By the time her clothing was put out, Maud was severely burned and died.

Uncle Charlie and Aunt Hattie looked for comfort from their family, their church and their community. They belonged to Mt. Carmel Baptist Church, which was located in Montieth Gap. Uncle Charlie was a deacon of the church until it closed its door in 1945. The family

walked the country mile to the church from their home in Peter's
Bluff. When Mt. Carmel closed its door, Uncle Charlie transferred his
membership to Liberty Baptist Church where he maintained his status
as a deacon.

To support his family, Uncle Charlie obtained a job at the Cullowhee Normal School, which was rapidly becoming a teachers' college. He retired from the college, which had become Western
Carolina Teachers' College. Like most of the Casey men, Uncle
Charlie knew his way around in the kitchen.

Education was important to the Charlie Casey family. He was
on the school committee for the black one-room school in Cullowhee.
His influenced continued into the 1950's when the school board made
the decision about the plans for a new school for the black children.
He was one of the black leaders who accepted and approved the plans
of the new building.

However, Uncle Charlie's generosity went beyond racial bound-
aries. In this mountainous county of Jackson, black and white folks
helped each other. When the Dills family needed money, Uncle Charlie gave them a loan. It was usually $20. He loaned money to other
families, both black and white.

Charity began at home and Uncle Charlie did his Christian duty.
His number one priority was the education of his children. Their
daughter, Ruth went to the Colored Consolidated School at Sylva in
1924. Afterward, she went to Allen Home to complete her high
school credits. Upon graduation from Allen in 1933, she eventually
went to Winston-Salem State Teachers' College in 1937. She graduated in 1942 and returned to Jackson County. She gave back to the
black community by teaching at Central Consolidated until 1944.

Their son, William went to the Colored Consolidated School in
Sylva and completed his high school credits at Lincoln Academy in
Black Mountain. With diploma in hand, he went to Detroit. He ob-
tained a job with the government and continued his schooling at
Wayne State College. When World War II erupted, he enlisted in the
Army. Uncle Charlie and Aunt Hattie were proud of their children.
Uncle Charlie continued to help his fellowman while Aunt Hattie
maintained their home, which set on a hillside in Peter's Bluff.

On December 6, 1957, Aunt Hattie passed away. After a year or
two, Uncle Charlie remarried...to a widow from Franklin, Mrs. Ella
Stewart Ledford. On September 28, 1965, Uncle Charlie passed. He

lived a long and fruitful life.

When the 911 system came in the county, the old dusty road where Uncle Charlie and other Casey's lived was named after him. The signed states Casey Road, but officially, it is the Charlie Casey Road on county maps.

My cousin Mary Sue Casey said of Uncle Charlie, "I thought he was rich the way he dressed when he came to church on Sunday." He was always decked out in dressed slacks and white shirt and tie. Most impressive was the girder he worn just above his elbow on his long sleeve dress shirt. He wore a bowler dress hat that sat cocked to the right. Rich or just styling! Maybe!

Rev. Joe H. Smith: A Servant to all
Tannery Flats

In August 1928, Rev. Joseph H. Smith became the pastor of Scotts Creek Liberty
Baptist Church. He was a native son of
Jackson County. His mother was Bessie Marjorie Love Smith and his grandfather was Mr.
Joe Smith. His grandfather was a slave and
told his grandson the treatment he received as
a slave.

Like most black children born in the
early nineteen hundreds, Rev. Joe H. Smith
was educated in the one-room segregated
black school in his district. Later, he attended
Calvary Presbyterian High School in Asheville and learned carpentry.
He stayed with Rev Anderson Wilson, who taught him the Bible.
Under his guidance, Joe became Rev. Joe H. Smith and was ordained
at age of 17. His first church was Rolland Chapel in Yancey County.

Now in the waning years of the roaring twenties, Rev Smith became the leader in his own community. He inherited Scotts Creek
Liberty Baptist Church built in 1906. As a young man, he had served
as janitor there.

The next year they began an addition to the church to accommo-
date the growing congregation. The addition was completed in 1930.
With the addition, they painted the outside and inside of the church.
Now the church proudly sat on the bank of Scotts Creek for all to see.

However, one Sunday morning as the 1930's were ending, Rev.
Smith noticed that the old part of the church and the new part were
coming apart. He knew it was time to raze the old structure and began
a new one. On May 28, 1940, they demolished the old church and
laid the foundation for a new building.

Two years later on the fourth Sunday in May, the congregation
marched into the church. They built the church out of rock –veneer
and concrete, which they hoped would last forever. Although this was
era that several black families moved north for economic reasons,
under the leadership of Rev. Smith, the membership continued to

grow.   Now members of Webster Baptist and Mt. Carmel Baptist of Cullowhee began to move their membership to Liberty.

Everything seemed to go smoothly as the church moved in the fifties in the wake of the Supreme Court decision on integration of schools. Then on January 10, 1958, Rev. Smith reminded his members that the church building was only a structure, his congregation was the church. That day after a funeral, fire destroyed Liberty Baptist.

Rev. Smith told the members to pray. After a period of prayer, some of the members gathered at Rev. Smith's home and worked on plans for another building. While they constructed another house of worship, they worshiped in the gymtoruim of Jackson School. A year later in April, they finalized the plans and began on another structure. On the last Sunday in December, the members marched into a new church home. They brick veneered the church in 1969 and today the structure still stands.

To show that Rev. Smith reached out to entire black community, he joined the Feast in the Wilderness, which

Mr. Jim Wells organized in about 1936. Rev. Joe Smith accepted the

invitation and all the black churches in county came together under one roof. The minutes for R. V. B. (River View Baptist) Church recorded that all the black churches in the county attended the Great Feast in the Wilderness on Sunday, July 30, 1939. Each church represented with a $1. Those churches were Webster, River View, Liberty, and A. M. E. Zion Churches.

However, by 1946, Liberty Baptist pulled out of the Feast in the Wilderness and started a Baptist Fifth Sunday Meeting. It was not because of domination, but Rev. Smith was pastoring Mount Olive Baptist in Canton, Mount Olive Baptist in Mars Hill, and Morning Star Baptist in Bryson City. With these churches, the Baptist Association formed their own.

Yet Rev. Smith served the entire black community of Jackson County. When his church held its Vacation Bible School, all the black communities were invited to come. Rev. Smith personally used his vehicle to transport children and adults to his church. He traveled to Cullowhee to pick up the Casey children and their mother, who provided the music for Vacation Bible School. He picked up other children in the Cullowhee area as well as others between Sylva and Cullowhee.

When the Civil Rights issue came close to Jackson County, Rev. Smith eased his congregation's mind on the subject. His easy laidback approach to his sermons played out in his social life. He always smiled and never raised his voice. His presence in the black community was always welcome as he reached out to all blacks. If there was any emergency, he was there to minister to the injury souls, whether they were Baptist or Methodist.

He served on boards in the county, which benefited the community. One of these boards was the Bryson Park Board. When integration was just around the corner, he was among the black leaders to approve the new black school in 1956. He and the others told the Board of Education that blacks were satisfied with the segregated system in the county.

Rev. Smith was not alone in his quest to service the black community. While he was pastor of Mount Olive Baptist in Mars Hill, the James Hampton family belonged to the church. They had a daughter, Syrilda Hampton. The young pastor, Rev. Smith, baptized Syrilda. Eventually, the couple dated and married. They moved to Sylva and lived with Mrs. Fredericka Love until they built their own home. The couple structured their home on the hill overlooking the church in the black Scotts Creek area. Dr. and Mrs. Joe H. Smith had one child, Marjorie.

After Marjorie grew up, Mrs. Syrilda went back to school and obtained her elementary education degree from Knoxville College. Before integration, Jackson County School System hired whites to work in Jackson School. After integration, Mrs. Syrilda obtained an assistant job in the library at Fairview Elementary. Realizing what was to come, she enrolled as a library major at Knoxville College. When the librarian retired, the school system hired her. In 1982, she retired after 19 1/2years of service.

Rev. Smith did a lot of evangelistic work across the United States. He broadcasted a radio show and worked in civic organizations. Traveling and preaching in foreign places, he visited Japan, the Holy Land, and Europe. For his dedicated Christian work, in 1982, he received an Honorary Doctor of Divinity Degree from Shaw University After retiring from the pulpit and social services, Dr. Smith's health began to decline; however, he continued to participate in funerals and other religious services.

On Sunday November 2, 1984, the church honored him with a day of appreciation. He had served the church for 54 years and the Waynesville Missionary Baptist Association for 50 years. Now the town of Sylva honored him for his contributions to the entire community of Jackson County. With the Bridge Park Project, he will forever be remembered as the black local Baptist preacher who served his community.

Of the six black churches in the county, he was the only pastor who resided in the community. Most of the other churches had itinerant pastors who lived just over the hill in Buncombe County, Swain County or far away as residing in Tennessee. Slowly the other Baptist churches in the county died and their members joined Liberty. Rev. Smith welcomed them and they became active members of the church.

On February 11, 1997, Dr. Rev. Joseph H. Smith passed away and Jackson County lost a dedicated humble citizen and Christian leader. He was the first African American to become a member of the Rotary Club in Jackson. One historian, Dr. Clifford Lovin said that Rev. Joe was the most important black person in the relationship between the white and black communities in the county.

Just Over the Hill

SECTION III
(1931-1950)
INTRODUCTION

B y 1930, the African American scattered communities had united as one. The consolidation of the segregated school system made all African American students attend the same school. The Feast in the Wilderness allowed all the African American churches to worship together each fifth Sunday.

It was stated that it was difficult to distinguish a Methodist from a Baptist, for each small African American community had both denominations. Within each community, the Methodist and the Baptist churches did not have service on the same Sunday. Each church arranged their programs around the programs of the other church in the community.

When there were Sunday School conventions, which lasted two or three days, the African American communities came together to house and feed the participates. Therefore, the stories in this section reflect the unity of the African American communities in Jackson County.

Within the unity of the African American communities, the respect for elders was apparent. In the school, all the male teachers were called Professor. We shorten that word to 'Fessor. All female teachers were called Miss. It did not matter if they were married or not. Some of the elderly African Americans ladies were called "Aunt" and the menfolk were addressed as "Uncle." This was out of respect for their wisdom. Sometimes their first name was used, but it was preceded with Mr. or Miss.

Uncle Smart: Hoodoo Man
Dillsboro/ Carter Cove

Back in the 1930's and 1940's young white boys like to camp out in the ridge between Rhodes Cove and Webster. One of their favorite spots was a little holler called Smart Carter Cove. In that cove was a spring and a crumbling foundation of a cabin. Those boys who went there wanted to know how the cove got its name. John Parris, the late author of the *"Roaming the Mountains"* column in the *Asheville Citizen* in his article on Mr. "Smart" Carter, he stated that he lived in that fallen cabin.

When Parris was teenager in the 1920's, Smart Carter was alive. John and his friends camped in Smart Carter Cove. They had to get water from Carter's spring. It seemed that they drew straws to see who was going to fetch the water. The boys were afraid of Carter because he had been taught the African art of healing.

One day, Carter saw one of the boys attempting to steal his water and he ran him off. He shouted and waved his hands in the air. This scared the boys. Afterward, they brought their own water supply.

Another time, some boys were caught stealing apples and Carter told them that they would turn into a tree. Vividly, he described the process. With no place to go, because they were in the apple tree, they had to listen. He told then that limbs would start coming out their mouths. Then the limbs would come out of their ears and nose. The next thing, you will be tied to the ground. Rooted there, they would soon to be a tree.

No one tampered with Carter's apples. For around these parts, he was a conjuring man who dabbled in hoodoo. The boys saw him dancing around in his yard, as he chanted in an unknown tongue. Sometimes, they heard him in the house chanting.

Some called him a root doctor, while other referred to him as a witch doctor. Some believed in his powers, other steered away from him. He made love portion from herbs, which he grew in his little garden. Those that believed came knocking at his door. It seemed that Carter kept the door bolted from the inside at all times.

It was well known that he was a hermit. Being a loner, his legend grew. The hoodoo man, who conjured up the spirits from the dead, had supernatural powers to bring the spirits and ghosts alive. Not only that, Carter wore a bear-claw necklace around his throat. Folks said that he stated that he wore it to keep the haunts away.

When he died, he had on his bear-claw necklace. Someone came

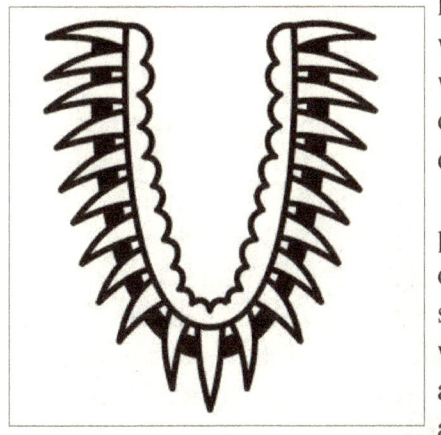

looking for some herbs...maybe it was a love portion. No matter what, they came. After knocking on the door, they found that Carter did not respond.

Fearing something had happened to him, they tried to open the door, but it was locked from the inside. They could not peep in the windows because all were closed and curtained. Hence, they pushed and pushed on the door until the bolt gave way. Lying in the bed, Carter was dead.

In the Parrish Cemetery, a marble tombstone stands. On this tombstone is name CARTER. In the county's cemetery book it is recorded S. Mart Carter. However, on the tombstone, there is no first or last name, just Carter. On the large two feet marble, C. J. Harris had this inscription. The epitaph reads:

REMEMBRANCE
Of
CARTER
FOR LONG YEARS
A FAITHFULL FRIEND
AND SERVANT
BY C. J. HARRIS

These words say a lot, but it does not answer the question who was Mr. Smart Carter?

In Minnie Gray's book on the history of Dillsboro, she listed the colored pioneers with their photograph. She wrote..."proved themselves to be worthy citizens," ...that meant that the colored pioneers served them as chambermaids, handymen, and washer women, a faithful friend or servant.

In the 1910 census, Mr. Carter resided in Harris's household in Dillsboro. There was no detail of his job. It simply recorded that he was a servant. Therefore, one can conclude that he was Colonel Harris's handyman.

Uncle Smart, however, did not arrived in Jackson with the Harris family. Mr. Harris was a northern industrialist, who came south after the Civil War. He employed Uncle Smart and when the servant became too old to work, he bought the land. When he settled in his little cove (which bore his name), he found the only spring within miles of the area. He built a one-room cabin where there were orchards of apple and peach trees and plenty of black scuppernong grapes.

The community believed he brought sickness and death, as well as healing. They had faith in his charms and his curative powers. Even some black folks said he made rag dolls to resemble folks. He stuck pins in the dolls to bring calamities to them, even death.

He was described as a little man, bent and old with his skin wrinkled and black as coal tar. It is said that he had Krumen blood and his folks came from the West Coast of Africa. Over the middle passage, they arrived in the New World and were put on the auction block, sold into slavery. Smart Carter became a product of that peculiar society.

Uncle Smart was born into slavery, but died a free landholder. He came to Western North Carolina in the late 1800's with Captain George Knight, who had been employed by the Richmond and Danville Railroad. Knight arrived here to supervise the bridge construction for the Murphy Division of the Richard/ Danville Railroad to connect with Western North Carolina Railroad. Knight brought his family and Uncle Smart was their household servant.

After Knight completed his assignment in 1891, he headed back to Virginia. Uncle Smart stayed and obtained a job with C. J. Harris. Carter was described in Parris's article of "Roaming the Mountains" as a major-domo to C. J. Harris.

When Uncle Smart retired, he went to the little cove on the land he bought. He built a cabin and began to practice his African healing art. For protection, he wore the bear claw necklace.

However, the photo which appeared in the Dillsboro history, portrayed him as a fashionable black man of his time. Smartly attired in a three-piece suit, a dress shirt and a tie, he gave the appearance of being a man of culture. Standing there, with his hat held in the crook of his arm, that image is complete. The white hair gives him a distinguished, sophisticated look. He seemed to be a perfect gentleman... not a hermit.

Civil Conservation Corps: Bob Bryson's Saving Grace
Tannery Flats

History records that the Civil Conservation Corps and its accomplishments had a lasting effect on Western North Carolina. There was large scale projects which kept lots of unemployed young men employed in CCC camps here in the mountain. The United States Forest Service specifically benefited from these projects. The Corps of men built roads and bridges, as well as planting forest and restoring watersheds.

This was the time of the Great Depression and impoverished families, as well as individuals, were unable to find employment. Therefore in 1933, the CCC camps were established under the Emergency Conservation Work Acts. It was just one of the many programs to alleviate the plight of the poor and unemployed.

In North Carolina 27 of 100 people were on relief. The hardest hit area was the mountain region. A report stated that close to three million men, between the ages of eighteen and twenty-five helped improve and preserve America's forests, parks and agricultural lands.

General George C. Marshall organized the Corps. Members lived in camps. They were required to wear uniforms and live under quasi-military discipline. Most who joined were malnourished and poorly clothed. Very few had a high school education. Their work experiences were mostly occasional odd jobs. To maintain a peaceful co-existence the threat of dishonorable discharge was held over their heads.

Some CCC camps were a row of army tents, while others were built like army barracks. The camp was located according to the terrain. In Jackson County, the CCC camp was situated between Dillsboro and Bryson City. All the enrollees had helped build the camp under the direction of United States Army officers.

The black and white enrollees from Jackson County had to build their own camp in this mountainous terrain. Among the African Americans who joined the CCC was Robert Bryson. He was born in the Tannery Flats area of Sylva on February 14, 1924. His parents were Mr. Ode and Mrs. Hattie Howell Bryson. At an early age, he joined Liberty Baptist Church.

By the time the ECW Acts were passed, Robert aka Bob was in need of a permanent job. He worked odd jobs around the Sylva area. With onset of the Depression, he desired to help out at home. He thought about joining the military, but CCC camp seemed like a better deal.

He had attended Colored Consolidated School. As he was promoted in the elementary department, he found himself skipping school. Finally after the eighth grade, he quit and began working at odd jobs around the county. The Tannery, where his father worked, was not hiring and the Mead Corporation did not hire African Americans. Therefore, Bob chose to join the CCC.

Upon enlisting, he found out he would make $30 a month and required to send at least $25 per month to his family. At last, Bob could help out at home where there were several mouths to feed.

When he arrived in camp, he realized they were going to build the CCC camp from the bottom up. The first building erected was the administration office and a flag pole so that Old Glory could fly proudly. Their construction job was the officers' barracks and the campers would be located behind the officers. Other buildings included latrines, hospital and infirmary, showers and washroom, kitchen and mess unit garage and shop.

Bob worked in the kitchen. He also helped with the restoration, the conservation, flood and fire control of the forest area of the Great

Smoky Mountains. Not only did these CCC provide work for the men, but educational opportunities through the Department of Education. For Bob Bryson and other blacks in the area, this camp was a saving grace.

When World War II began he entered the military. He joined the United States Navy and worked in the galley as a cook. After the war was over, he married Margie Fisher and began work at Sunset Farm. Using his Navy skills, he became the head cook. Later, he obtained employment at Cagle & Son Ford. He remained there until retirement.

On November 2, 1998, Bob passed away at Harris Regional Hospital after a short illness. Mr. Robert "Bob" Bryson served his country when he was needed. By joining the CCC, he helped preserve the national forest in North Carolina and by joining the U. S. Navy he defended his country.

The Sylva Women's Club
Tannery Flats

In the 1930's when the Great Depression had folks homeless, jobless and penniless, the black women of Jackson County formed a sewing club. Mrs. Mattie K. Shepeard organized it. In the beginning, its members were women from in and around Sylva. They met once a month at a member's home. They looked at the housing situation and addressed some solution to the problem. Their aim was to help the needy blacks in the Sylva area.

Members of the club were Mrs. Syrilda Smith, Mrs. Grace

Bryson, Mrs. Carrie Davis, Mrs. Virginia Wilson, Mrs. Fredrick Love, Mrs. May Bryson, Mrs. Otylia Studderth, Mrs. Annie Dorsey, Mrs. Mamie Curry, and Mrs. Janie May Whittenburg.

Mrs. Mattie K., founder of the organization, was a member of Liberty Baptist Church. She was an excellent organizer and knew how to make the black women feel important. With this sewing club, it gave them a sense of community. The women from the Tannery Flats were able to sat down with the women of Scotts Creek to address the black problem.

In the beginning, it was called the Sewing Club. This sewing circle gave the women status in their community. They all belonged to Liberty Baptist, which meant they were leaders in the black community. From this organization, a black Girl Scouts troop formed with Mrs. Grace as the leader. They gave scholarships to black students, who aspired to further their education beyond high school.

By the 1940's, the club changed its name to the Sylva Women Club. The depression had passed and Roosevelt had given the nation hope. Now the club took on new leaf. With ease of traveling to Cullowhee to Sylva, they invited other women to the club. The membership was no longer the exclusive organization of Liberty Baptist Church in the Sylva area, but those in Cullowhee, also.

The 100th Anniversary booklet of the church listed the club as an auxiliary; therefore, they always began their meeting with a spiritual song and a prayer.

Here is a report of a February 21, 1957 meeting that Mrs. Virginia Wilson addressed to the Sylva Herald for Negro News:

"The Women's Club met at the home of Mrs. O. Studderth. It was opened by singing "Near the Cross," followed by prayer by Rev. Marie Hayward. After the business, a short program was rendered. The hostess served a delicious sweet course carrying on the Valentine motif with both shapes and color. The prize was won by Mrs. Mamie Curry."

During the 1950's the Negro News became the source of the happenings in the black neighborhoods and each month Mrs. Virginia reported on the Women's Club. Each month different members would entertain the club at their homes. After the business meeting, there was a short program and refreshments. Sometimes, there would be a guest speaker to give them insight on politic or social situations in the county.

As time went by and integration took over the black schools, the club slowly died. Migrations contributed to the demise, as well as death of the members.

Miss Mamie Davis and the Flood of 1940
Lower River Road

Mr. and Mrs. Robert Davis were one of the most respected colored couple in Cullowhee. A fixture on the campus of Cullowhee Normal School, which evolved into a four-year teacher's college, Mr. Robert began working for the founder of the school Professor Robert Madison. Professor Madison hired this small boy to do various chores around the campus. One day the young lad killed a large turtle, but it was too heavy for him to carry it up the steps.

After being a small hired hand for Madison, Mr. Robert started a hack line service, which accommodated the needs of the ever-growing college. He ran a hack line from Sylva to Cullowhee, which usually took about three hours. He hauled wood with his sled and one horse wagon, as well as transporting students from Sylva's depot to Cullowhee and vice versa. While operating his hack line, he met and married Mamie Summerford from eastern part of North Carolina in 1914. Miss Mamie was hired as a housekeeper for students who were coming from afar. Therefore, the school built dormitories to accommodate the students.

In 1925, Mr. Robert became the head janitor and Mrs. Mamie became the head housekeeper. The couple enjoyed their status in the white community as well as the black community. In the black community, she was known as Mrs. Mamie, while the white community even the students she served called her Mamie. It was the same with Mr. Robert. He was simply Robert.

It did not matter to them. They had good jobs and a home on their own land given to them by Mr. Thomas Davis, Mr. Robert's fa-

114

ther.   On lower river road (Casey Road), the Davises built their home. The two-story white framed house was Mrs. Mamie's pride and joy. She kept their home spic and span and displayed for anyone who visited her. She managed to work as the head housekeeper at the college and to rear three children.

In their home, Mrs. Mamie listened to Mr. Robert as he recalled his hectic day as the head janitor. Always jingling from his belt loop of his trouser was a set of keys. Before he entered a room, the keys could be heard.

She can remembered the day he came home to tell her about the safe he was to transport to the college from the Sylva depot. They had discussed it and thought it would be best to take a wagon driven by four mules. When he got home that night at the dinner table, there was laughter. Everyone had expected a huge heavy safe, but the safe was very small. Other times, Mr. Robert drove students to parties off campus and she would wait up for him. Those were the good times as Mr. Robert gave her an hour-by-hour account of the event.

August of 1940 brought some changes. Heavy rain continued for weeks. The Tuckaseigee River begam to rise. There had never been a flood on the Tuckaseigee and Mrs. Mamie could not see her home flooded. She was convinced that a flood would not occur. On the night of August 30, all hell broke loose. No one really knew what happened, but most said it was a "cloudburst." At any rate, the Tuckaseigee flooded with the water closing in on the Davis' home.

Robert got the children to safety, but Mamie would not go. She looked around at her beautiful home. The water would stop, but it continued to surround the house of her dreams. The water did not crest, but proceeded to flood the bottom floor. Water was swirling around her feet. The upper floor would be her refuge. Mr. Robert returned to help Mamie escape the rapidly rising water.   In her arms, Mrs. Mamie clutched her silverware.

Roaring in his ears was the angry Tuckaseegee. This was no time to argue, but to act. Mr. Robert promised Mamie that he would build her house on the top of the hill as he bodily picked up her and carried her to safety. As they climbed the bank, the water engulfed most of the downstairs and the Tuckaseigee was moving the house from its foundation.

After the flood, Mr. Robert and Mrs. Mamie relocated their home on the hill high above the Tuckaseegee. He made good his promise.

This is the new house Robert Davis promised his wife Mamie after the 1940 flood. It was built just over the hill from the other house. This picture of the 1956 Kemp-Davis family reunion was taken in front of their new home.

Migrating North: The James Robert Casey, Sr. Story
Cullowhee/Bryson City/Lima, Ohio

With the depression of the late thirties and the coming of World War II, many African Americans in Jackson County began to migrate to the North. Employment was hard to find and wages were too low to raise a family. Hard times hit everyone. One of these individuals was James Robert Casey. Born on April 16, 1915, he was the sixth son of Mr. George and Mrs. Sadie Jane Hooper Casey.

He attended the segregated school system in Jackson County, beginning school in 1921 and attending the one room school in Cullowhee before he transferred to Sylva when the Cullowhee Colored School Committee voted to allow their children to be bussed to Sylva. Like his brothers, he belonged to the MethoBapist churches in Cullowhee. In other words, he attended both black churches in Cullowhee (Mt. Carmel Baptist Church and AME Zion Mt. Zion Church).

After graduating from the tenth grade, he attempted to find employment in the area. Jobs were scarce in Jackson County; therefore he headed toward Bryson City in the late 1930's. Rumor had it that the Tennessee Valley Authorities were going to build a dam across the Little Tennessee River in Swain County and Graham County. James knew the situation in Graham County. Therefore he stopped in Swain County.

While in Swain County, he met Miss Mattie Simpson, who was the daughter of Mr. Lake and Mrs. Marie Simpson of Asheville. The family moved from Buncombe County when Mattie was about eight years old. She attended the segregated school system of Swain County and transferred to Allen Home in Asheville. However, meeting the handsome James halted her pursuit to continue her studies.

In the meanwhile, James sought steady employment. It seemed that TVA was dragging their feet. However it was not TVA who was holding up progress, but ALCOA. It was rumored that this dam needed to be built to accommodate the demand of electricity in the Tennessee Valley. A lot of people were going to be removed from their homes to make way for this progress.

Finally on April 14, 1941, TVA and ALCOA signed an agreement, which gave TVA the authority to begin hiring and finding housing for thousands of workers. A majority of these men came from Western North Carolina. Preparation of the project began. Among those who were hired was James Robert. Pay was not much, but they worked a seven day week schedule. Pay was about $5 a week without any overtime. That meant there would be three shifts a day. When one crew finished for the day, another crew stepped in to complete the job. Those who work the third shift, labored under flashlights.

James was not afraid of work. He was brought up working hard. It seemed as soon as he could walk, he worked in the fields at home. As boy growing up, his father hired him out to white farmers. Working by the sweat of his brow, he learned to be a welder, and as a welder, he felt he could make more money and marry Mattie.

However, things got out of control before he could get situated. Mattie reported to James that she was pregnant. James knew it was his child and he also knew that Mattie's father would not be happy. Marriage was the only sensible thing to do. Mattie's mother was dead. She died when Mattie was about ten years old. There was not only Mattie to consider, but Mattie had a baby sister, Alice Louise. She was in boarding school at Allen Home in Asheville. During the school year she was at school, but during breaks, she returned and Mattie looked after her.

Things had to change. James continued to work and tried to save some money. In this tiny town, James heard that up North they were looking for able-bodied men to work in the factories. Most of the northern men were at War on the front line.

Older men from up North were saying that Ohio Steel Foundry was hiring skilled individuals. One of the skills was welding. James couldn't believe that. This was his opportunity to move north.

On his day off, he went home and talked about it to his older brothers, Estus and Henry. Perhaps, the three could go north together.

It seemed right. Henry had a good job at Western Carolina Teacher College and he did not want to make the move.

However, on the other hand, Estus who had recently quit his job at Western seemed to think it was a great idea. James returned to Bryson City to tell Mattie of his plans. The two would get married. He would go on to the little town of Lima and hopefully obtain a job as a welder at the Ohio Steel Foundry.

During the same time that TVA was awarding funds for Fontana Dam Project, the United States Army developed a plan to utilize the Foundry. It was a government-owned plant to manufacture centrifugally-cast gun tubes for Army tanks. Lima, Ohio was chosen because of its proximity to five railroads and national highway routes.

The construction of the dam had begun on January 1, 1942, after being funded on December 17, 1941 by Congress.

It was June, 1942 when Mattie and James got married. James quit his job and hopped a ride to Lima, Ohio. It seemed that Estus's wife had convinced Estus that it would not be practical. There was no way that he could live there and save enough money to bring all their seven children up there. Therefore, James went alone. On October 15, Mattie gave birth to a son. She named him James Robert Casey, Jr. They called him Bobby. When Alice Louise was dismissed for Christmas vacation, Mattie with Bobby and her sister Alice Louise hopped a bus and traveled to Lima, Ohio. James met them at the bus station and the rest is history

This is just one of the stories of African Americans migrating to the North to find a better place for his family. James and Mattie had two other children. Judy Marie was born in 1946 and Kenneth was born in 1947.

Family was important to James and Mattie. They always visited Western North Carolina to connect with their family in Jackson and Swain counties.

Gossip Columnists or News Reporters!
River View/Tannery Flat

Katherine Love Wells

During World War II, *The Church and Southland Advocate,* an Asheville based black daily newspaper, permitted Western North Carolina black communities to have a column in its paper. From Jackson County, two black communities sent weekly news to the paper. From Dillsboro, Mrs. Katherine Love Wells wrote the column, which was full of happenings in the River View / Dillsboro and Webster areas.

In the Sylva area, Mrs. Mary Babb and Mrs. Jane Whittenburg provided the happening in and around Sylva and Cullowhee. If there was an archive of that newspaper, one could read about births, marriages, engagements, deaths and other social events. Just a visit out of town was recorded or who was invited to Sunday dinner.

However, most important was the church news. It was always written with details, especially the Feast in the Wilderness. The report on the church service was first item, because both the reporters were churchgoers.

Mrs. Katherine Love Wells was the wife of Mr. Jim Wells, the founder of the Feast. She belonged to River View Baptist Church. In October 15, 1946 issue of the Advocate, Mrs. Katherine reported that on September 9, Rev. J. C. McElrath opened his fall revival with Rev. A. H. Wilson as the conductor. The revival lasted for five days and both races attended the services.

She wrote of the services, *"Each message was filled with the*

*Holy Ghost and was a bread cast upon the water and will be gathered
many days hence." She even reported the total finance, which was
$61 for the week.*

*Both ministers were from out of town, therefore, they resided with
one of the members of River View. They made their home with Mrs.
Zellia Wells, who was Mrs. Katherine's mother-in-law.*

*Although they stayed at Mrs. Zellia, they dined at different mem-
bers' home during their weekly stay. On Monday they dined at Mr.
and Mrs. J. W. Wells (Mrs. Katherine's home), on Tuesday they dined
at Mr. and Mrs. A. L. Pettit , on Wednesday they dined at Mr. and Mrs.
Dock Love, on Thursday they dined at Mr. and Mrs. J. W. Evans and
on Friday they dined at Mr. and Mrs. J. P. England.*

*Rev. McElrath held regular services on Sunday, September 15. It
was an all-day event with a Baptismal service held that afternoon.
Richard Alston of Cullowhee was baptized. Out of town visitors from
Cullowhee, Sylva and Asheville attended the event.*

*That night Rev. McElrath chose for a text Mark 1:11. Everyone
enjoyed the sermon, especially the white people who expressed it as
the greatest sermon they had ever heard. The collection for that day
was $48.37.*

*Webster did not have services on September 22. It seemed that
the Church Convention was in session."*

Is this a gossip column or news? Between reporting about church
services, Mrs. Katherine writes about who visited who. Just by reading this column, the names of black folks who lived in Jackson
County come alive. Not gossip, but truth, which told the next generation who was living there before the northern migration.

Next to last item in this column was the report on the 30th ses-
sion of the Feast in the Wilderness, which convened at River View
Baptist Church. After that, she reported where Rev. and Mrs. B. T.
Turner and Rev. and Mrs. J. C. McElrath dined. They ate at her home.

The Sylvia (Sylva) News written by Mary A. Babb had the same
tone in her column. Mrs. Babb was member of Scott Creek Liberty
Baptist Church where her husband Brother William Babb helped lead
devotion for the Fifth Sunday Union meeting.

By reading Mrs. Babb's column, one realized that Liberty Baptist
had their own fifth Sunday gathering and they called it Fifth Sunday
Union. The churches which attended these meetings were all Baptist

churches. Besides Liberty, New Hope Baptist of Knoxville and Pleasant Grove of Canton were present.

Unlike Mrs. Katherine, her descriptions were brief of the activities of the meeting. However, like Mrs. Katherine, she reported about the tragedies and the triumphs of the black home folks in Sylva and Cullowhee. On one day in June 1948, she began with sad news: *"Mr. Grant Wilson died May 15. He was a member of Maize Chapel. Mrs. Jessie Casey of Cullowhee is the hospital in Asheville and Mrs. Theodore Lackey is still very ill.*

School is out and Isabell Howell and Marine Whittenburg have returned home from Allen High School in Asheville. Margaret Streater of Cullowhee, Ruby and Hazel Bryson of Sylva are home from college. Club La-Phare performed at Central Consolidated for May Day on May 26. Miss Angelina McDowell and Charles Sudderth married on May 20."

All important news items kept the African American public informed.

In the Sylva News column written by Mrs. Jane Whittenberg in February of 1945, she reported on the Fifth Union Meeting of Sylva, Waynesville and Canton, which was held at Liberty Baptist on Sunday, December 31, 1944. Unlike, the report on the Feast in the Wilderness by Mrs. Katherine, she did not go into any lengthy details. It was all day event with evening service. Like the Feast, it had a program, which Miss Edith Casey was mistress of ceremony. Rev. E. E. Burnside delivered the morning message, while Rev. J. C. Conley delivered the afternoon message and Rev. Roscoe Burgess delivered the evening message.

From her report, she stated the following:

"Each sermon preached was both Spiritual and inspiring. The public responded to the call of finance of the day in a very commendable way. Amount collected was $67."

Most of her news was centered on Liberty Baptist, which Mr. Whittenberg was a member. She is the wife of Mr. McKinley Whittenberg, a deacon at the church. Maize Chapel AME Zion was mentioned in short paragraph for January 21, 1945. Their pastor Rev. B. T. Turner delivered the messages at each service. His subject for the afternoon service was "What Will I Do without Jesus?"

Like the other column, she reported on illness and who visited whom. Her last item reported that Pvt. James Ray Pettit, son Mr. and

Mrs. A. L. Pettit was killed accidentally in France.

When the Advocate folded and the 1950's came, Mrs. Virginia Wilson wrote Negro News in the local newspaper, The Sylva Herald. She was the wife of Mr. Charlie Wilson. They lived in the Tannery Flats and were members of Maize Chapel.

It appeared that all the white communities had a column for their news, and the black folks did the same. Mrs. Virginia had to gather news from all the little hamlets where black folks lived. She began a 1950's article with the second quarterly conference held at Maize Chapel on February 16 and 17. We learn that on Sunday morning the Presiding Elder spoke and Rev Marie Hayward pastor of the church spoke that afternoon.

Her next item was Silver Tea sponsored by the PTA of Jackson School. It was held Sunday afternoon and it was well attended. The proceeds went to the lunchroom for supply.

All though the article, she reported on the happening in the different churches. The Missionary Circle of Mt. Zion in Cullowhee met on Wednesday night, February 13. Mrs. DeRosette Casey attended the first mass meeting in Tennessee. Rev. J. H. Sullivan was at River View Baptist. The Missionaries of Liberty Baptist went to Waynesville Sunday to a district meeting.

She reported to her audience that the sick were recovering. The sick listed included Aunt Zelia Wells, Mrs. Janie M. Whittenburg, Mr. Jess Howell and Mrs. Alma Coward.

From church to the sick to social gathering to sports, Mrs. Virginia covered all of it. Just as Mrs. Katherine and Mrs. Babb recorded history, so did Mrs. Virginia.

Miss DeRosette Casey: First PTA President of CHS

Peter's Bluff

In 1948, Central Consolidated High School organized a PTA and elected Mrs. DeRosette Casey as president. Mrs. DeRosette was not from Jackson County, but just over the hill in Buncombe County. Born in Charlotte, North Carolina in August of 1906, she was the daughter of Mr. Elias Charles Blaylock and Mrs. Mary Mamie Asbury Horne. When she was a little girl, the family moved to Asheville where DeRosette and her brothers grew up in segregated neighborhoods. They obtained their education through the segregated school system.

On graduating from high school, she attended Knoxville College to obtain a teaching degree. Upon graduation on May 19, 1925, she received a Standard Teacher Training Course diploma. During the summers of 1925 to 1929, DeRosette attended summer school to obtain credit to teach in North Carolina. The Department of Public Instruction awarded her a Class B Elementary Teacher's Certificate in 1927 and a Class A Elementary Teacher Certificate in 1929.

She obtained her first contract on July 14, 1928 to teach in Buncombe County in the Limestone Township at Arden Colored School. She taught for three years.

In 1931 she went just over the hill to Swain County to teach in the Charleston Township. According to the contract, she had taught for six years and was paid $48 a month.

124

While teaching there, she met her future husband George Estus Casey. They perhaps met at a juke joint because DeRosette loved to dance. Estus courted her and she visited his home in Montieth Gap. The city girl and country boy married on April 28, 1934 in Sylva.

After she was married, she devoted most of her time rearing nine children and orchestrating their education. DeRosette joined Mt. Zion AME Zion Methodist Church in Cullowhee where Estus was a member. She grew up in Berry Temple CM Methodist Church in Asheville. Therefore, it was not difficult for her to become an active member. An excellent piano player, she became the church pianist and kept that position until she joined Maize Chapel in the Tannery Flats in the late 1960's. She went to church regularly, unless there was some altercation with the pastor. Working in the church, she organized programs for the different occasions. Being a schoolteacher, she worked with the children and some of them remember the programs were well organized

On August 18, 1934, she wrote a letter to Presiding Elder J. W. Hill about some misappropriation of church funds by the pastor of Jones Temple. It seemed that she and others were on the Investigating Committee when the District Conference met at Sylva from August 15- 19.

When she became the president of the PTA, DeRosette organized the parents, especially the mothers. She appointed Grade Mothers at the different department levels. There were Grade Mothers for the Primary Department, Elementary Department and the High School Department. Their number one job description was to establish friendly relations with parents and procure from the teacher or principal the names, addresses of the parents whose children were enrolled in the room and to keep them for reference.

She organized a City Service Committee whose job description included to assist in the nationwide effort to provide qualified teachers for the schools. This committee consisted of the fathers and headed by Rev. Joe H. Smith, pastor of Liberty Baptist Church.

Another important committee was the Publicity Committee whose job was to send news release, notices, bulletins and announcements to the newspaper. To do that, she told them they had to make the acquaintance of the editor, reporters, and publicists

DeRosette wrote jobs description to all her committees. At the beginning of the second year of their existence, DeRosette wrote a memo to the school. She documented their accomplishments. They had purchased bioscopes and slides for the science department, a world globe for the elementary department, and a hectograph for the primary department. The Grade Mothers gave pencils, soap, paper, and magazines. They also organized a party for all their different groups. Their project that year was to purchase typewriters for the business department and the mission was accomplished.

To make the PTA legit, she had the organization to join the North Carolina Congress of Colored Parents and Teachers, Inc.

On October 28, 1948, she went to see Supt. W. Vernon Cope on the matter of the rumors being circulated in the Black communities. Several Blacks were complaining about the teachers and the school. In her conference with Supt. Cope, he said, "You have the best run school and the best teachers (excluding none in the county). Wade and Frank have good certificates and working on their Master's Degree. Lockwood Love is well-qualified and a perfect gentleman. You need not worry for I, the Board and the Committee are backing the school and the teachers 100%, for they are fine."

On April 16, 1955, she led a group discussion on the topic "Interpreting the School to the Community" at the District PTA meeting in Brevard. The postcard which she received from Mrs. Arney Johnson stated, "We hope you won't say "no," for your capabilities are rated high on the list."

In 1965 at the last graduating exercise at the school, she delivered the invocation. She had seen the school go through many changes. From the plank structure, which did not have indoor plumbing or central heating to the brick structure with indoor plumbing and central heating. She had worked in the school to make a different.

Seven of her nine children graduated from the all black school in Jackson County. Whether it was college or a trade school, most of them pursued a higher education. Two of her children attended all black colleges in North Carolina. Delaney, her oldest son attended Johnson C. Smith in Charlotte and her oldest daughter Permelia attended North Carolina Central in Durham. She graduated cum laude.

Medford, her second son, finished his high school education at Stephen Lee High in Asheville. Geraldyne, her second oldest daughter, graduated high school with Permelia at the new all black school Jackson High in Sylva. She went to Asheville. There, she attended and graduated from the Stewart's School of Beauty Culture. After graduating, she applied her trade as a beautician at a beauty salon in Asheville.

Her middle child, Lorinda graduated from high school and eventually went to work as a domestic servant in and around Sylva, as well as the Asheville area. Upon returning to Cullowhee, she obtained a job at Western Carolina University (WCU), where she took classes along with other classes at Southwestern Tech.

The twins, Victor and myself, pursued correspondent courses. Victor went to Chicago and started a broadcasting course and I took a correspondent art course with Famous Artists School, as well as a correspondent writing course. Victor was drafted into the army and sent to Vietnam as a communication operator and at the same time I had received a job as a switchboard operator at the local telephone company.

Eventually, I went to WCU and graduated in the summer of 1973. In the meanwhile, Irma graduated from Jackson high school, and Floretta graduated from Camp Lab in Cullowhee. They both graduated from WCU before I did. Irma graduated cum laude with a psychology major. She worked in Greenville, North Carolina as social worker. Floretta and I followed our mother's example and became elementary school teachers.

A Call to Duty: Private Ida Jean Allen
Hog Rock

On December 7, 1941, as the American people listened to their radios on this Sunday morning when the regular broadcast was interrupted with the announcement that the Japanese had attacked Pearl Harbor. Many American lives were lost, as the Japanese airplane destroyed ships and airplanes of the United States Pacific fleet.

We, the American people, declared war on the Japanese, thus legally engaging in World War II. There was a call to duty as many American men volunteered themselves as they rushed to the recruiting office in their area to enlist in the armed forces to defend the United States democracy.

In this mountainous area of Western North Carolina, many answered the call. Some were too young and had to have their parents' signature before entering the adventure that some thought was glamorous and they could become a "knight in shining armor." Not only that, the airplane itself enticed many young men, with African Americans and whites aspiring to become "fighting aces." However, this story is not about the men, but it is about one of the African American women in the military.

The development of the WAC (Women's Army Corps) was a huge step in supporting the men. By no means did these women fight, but were trained to work in the office, in the hospitals, or in the fields as ambulance drivers or nurses in MASH units.

Young African American girls who were becoming independent women, found that being in the WAC was a chance to help their country and to leave the small community where they lived. However, like their counterparts, their parents had to sign if they had not reached the magic age of 21. Not only did these young ladies have to be 21, they had to have no dependents, be five-feet tall and weigh at least 100 pounds.

One of these girls, Ida Jean Allen, grew up in the small hamlet of Hog Rock in Jackson County. Her parents were W. Lawrence and Hattie Allen. When she finished her schooling at Central Consolidated School in Sylva, she worked as a domestic servant in white folks homes. Leaving Jackson County, she went to Waynesville to live with an aunt. Perhaps in Haywood County, she could find better opportunities. At any rate, she did not lose contact with her friends and family in Jackson County for Waynesville in Haywood County was just over hill (Balsam Mountain).

As America declared war on Japan and their allies, she was at war with herself. A new world awaited her outside of Western North Carolina. She discussed this opportunity with her friends Willie Grace Austin, Annie Lee Freeman, Martha Jean Bryson, Essie Love and others. At the time, some of the young ladies had not reached that magic age of 21. Each knew their parents had to sign them to enlist in the WACs. Some were willing to go and they decided to enlist.

Returning to her home county of Jackson, Ida Jean Allen enlisted in Women's Army Corps at the Sylva office. It was now 1944, but she still was not 21. Therefore, she went to her father and he signed the paper for her to enlist. Other African Americans had attempted to join the WACs, but they had been turned down. Therefore, Ida Jean Allen decided to challenge the system one more time. After all, some of her girl friends were enlisting with her.

On the morning of her departure from Sylva on the passenger train of the Western North Carolina Railroad, she realized her girlfriends had changed their minds. She was alone, but an acquaintance from Bryson City had enlisted and the ride to Fort Devan, Massachusetts would not be a lonely one.

When they reached Fort Devan, Ida found herself among other African American small town girls who wanted to make a difference. They were all now in the United States Army. They packed their civilian clothes and donned the uniform of the WAC. For the next two years, they took commands from their superiors. Life was not their own. No more getting up late to get their beauty sleep, but they had to rise as reveille called. Basic training had begun. Ida realized that her life was changing. The military was not all fun and games. Like a slave, one had to obey orders. Perhaps, Ida thought about what her parents had gone though as slaves. Yet, there was a difference. She would be paid for her services and she could terminate her services after two years. Now Ida was Private Ida Jean Allen.

Pvt. Allen remained at Fort Devan for almost a year, and then she and her unit were transferred to Fort Des Moines, Iowa. When her unit got there, they found that another African American unit was already there. Within a week, they transferred to Walla Walla, Washington and on to Fort Riley, Kansas. It seemed that she traveled across the United States and back again. Her unit remained at Fort Riley until they shipped out overseas. Unfortunately, Pvt. Allen missed the opportunity to go oversea. After training for overseas duty, she went home to the mountains on a furlough. While she was gone, her unit shipped out.

Therefore, Pvt. Allen remained at Fort Riley until her discharge. She worked in the hospital, attending the wounded soldiers. She talked to them and comforted them. She wrote letters dictated to her by the wounded. Pvt. Allen tried to make a difference in these soldiers' lives.

Fort Riley was not all work and no play. While there, she met Cpl. Clarence Turner and the two dated. He was from Birmingham. One of her friends was also from Birmingham. When Pvt. Allen was honorably discharged in 1946, she went to Alabama with her friend Calene Watt.

Cpl. Turner returned home. They resumed their relationship and he asked her to marry him. They married and a year later their first son, Clarence, Jr. was born. The couple stayed at Turner's childhood home with his mother. No longer, a private in the army, Ida Turner did not like the fact that Clarence did not attempt to get a job.

Now pregnant with her second child, Ida decided to come home for a visit. Clarence's mother persuaded Ida to leave Clarence Jr. with her. Ida left and never returned. She and Clarence eventually got a divorce. Jackie, her second child grew up in Sylva, while Clarence Jr. remained in Birmingham. Over the years, Clarence Jr. visited his mother, who married John Robert Bryson and mothered three more children, Robbie, Mike and Tammy.

For Ida Jean Allen Turner Bryson, there were good memories of Fort Riley. While there, she had many friends, such as J. D. Rendels, Mary Jyles, Montina Monroe, Orela Lee Waffer, Edith Elletos, Pvt. Meldered Hoke, Florence Johnson, Minnie Lasseter, Hazel Jackson,

Virginia Collins, Lt. Gates, Cpt. Alston, Pfc. Annie B. Jackson, Jo Jean Bettye, Istella S. Brooks and Freda W.

During this time, Joe Louis was the heavyweight champion of the world and Sugar Ray Robinson was the welterweight champion. Both men joined the army and became ambassadors for the army. Pvt. Allen met them while stationed at Fort Riley.

Although Pvt. Allen missed an opportunity to go overseas, she answered the call to duty by serving in the WAC's from 1944 to 1946.

Above, Ida Jean with Joe Louis, and on the right, Ida Jean with Sugar Ray Robinson

The Pettit Brothers: Serving their Country
River View

In 1941 when the United States declared war on Japan and the
other Axis Power during World War II, five brothers joined the
armed forces to fight to save democracy. The president of the
United States did not declare that this was "a white man's war," but
one to save the democratic governments around the world. America's
Pacific fleet had all but been wiped out at Pearl Harbor and a black
sailor stood in the gap. Dorie Miller dragged his dying captain away
from the shelling and operated a machine gun at the Japanese in-
vaders.

Therefore, the five brothers decided to join the armed forces.
Two of them selected the United States Navy, while one selected the
United States Air Force and the other two selected the United States
Army. Who were these five young Black men from Jackson County?
They were the sons of Reverend Abraham and Nina Pettit, who
resided in River View Community a sub-section of Dillsboro.

Like all the black families in the county, the Pettits wanted their
children to be educated. The five sons along with their other siblings
attended Central Consolidated School in Sylva. They participated in
basketball and other extra curriculum activities. When they graduated
from the tenth grade, their parents sent them to other black schools in
the area, like Lincoln Academy and Cherryville High School.

Willard Pettit joined the US Navy and served in Hawaii. Abraham Pettit joined the Air Force with his friend Clifford Casey.
George and James Ray Pettit served overseas in France. Argyle Pettit
joined the US Navy and served on USS Essex in the Pacific.

Private James Ray was in the engineer corps of the Army. While
in France, he was caught in an air raid from the Axis Power and
killed. He was the first black soldier killed in World War II from
Jackson County.

The Pettits got the news from the captain of the recruiting office
in the county. He walked all the way to the Pettits home on the hillside of River View to deliver the news personally. It was just a few
days before Christmas.

When the conflict ended, Seaman Argyle was stationed aboard

the USS Missouri flagship of the of United States Pacific fleet. General Douglas MacArthur the Supreme Commander of Allied Forces in the Southwest Pacific signed the surrender documents with Japanese General Yoshihito Umezu on board the USS Missouri. Seaman Argyle stood guard as the two parties signed the documents of surrender.

Four of the Pettit boys came home to a hardy, but sad welcome from their parents. Unlike the movie "Saving Private Ryan," the military did not have to save the last of Rev. and Mrs. Pettit's sons. Although they served behind the enemy lines, four returned home.

On grounds of the old Court House in Sylva, James Ray Pettit's name appears on a memorial plaque as a casualty of World War II.

The 30th Session of the Feast in the Wilderness
River View

On Sunday September 29, 1946, the 30th session of the Feast in the Wilderness convened at River View Baptist in the River View section of Dillsboro. Cars parked down the hill from the church, which set on a knoll. The unpaved road left dust as the cars sped toward the church. Dressed in their Sunday best, they came from near and far.

The regular crowd from Cullowhee and Sylva came as they represented their churches, Maize Chapel and Mt Zion. Both churches belonged to the AME Zion Methodist Churches and the Blue Ridge Conference considered them a circuit. It was called the Mt. Zion Circuit and one pastor served both churches on alternating Sundays. Their pastor, Rev. B. T. Turner came from Asheville, as did River View's pastor Rev. J. C. McElrath.

Sunday school had already dismissed by the time some of the follows got there. The Estus Casey family arrived just in time for morning service. There was Delaney, Medford, Permelia, Geraldyne, Lorinda, Victoria, Victor and eight-month-old baby girl, Floretta. Mother, father and children sat in the middle row near the front.

The church began to fill up as folks from Hog Rock and Webster arrived. The house became crowded as some people from Bryson City came to hear one of their own deliver the morning message.

The president, Mr. Jim Wells presided over the morning session. Everyone knew that the Holy Ghost spirit would electrify the mass as the old hymns filled the air with joy. Before the morning ended, everyone anticipated that Mr. Jim would sing one of his favorites *"Somebody Touched Me."* He did, just before Rev. Wade Howell of Bryson City delivered the morning sermon. Amidst all of praising the Lord, the scripture where Rev. Howell obtained his sermon was John 1: 1-9 and his subject was "The Light of the World."

After the morning session, everyone ate at the church. Church members brought fried chicken, potato salad, green beans, sweetbread and pies of all kind. Aunt Zettie's sweet potato custard pie was Uncle Henry's favorite dessert. Most folks ate outside. They stood with plates in hand or found a spot to sit down on the grass. Some families with small children ate in the back of the church.

Before the afternoon sermon, at 2:30 the youth and elders showed their talent though song or poetry. Albert Davis, son of Mr. and Mrs. Robert Davis sang *"Our Father,"* followed by a selection from the Estus Casey children with their mother Mrs. DeRosette Casey accompanying on the piano. While still seated at the piano, Mrs. Casey tickled the ivory for her twins to sing a duet. At the tender age of three, Victor and I made our stage debut by singing *"Jesus Loves Me."* Miss Carolyn Shepherd, daughter of Mr. and Mrs. Hubert Shepherd of Sylva sang *"Holy Spirit."* Mrs. Virginia Wilson of Maize Chapel read "You're Going to Reap What You Sow." Mrs. Alda Bowie and Miss Orba Love, daughters of Mr. and Mrs. Dock Love, sang a duet. (Mrs. Bowie and her son, Jimmie from Arkansas were visiting her parents.) A quartet from Little Savannah rendered a song. The group consisted of Mrs. Annie Belle Fisher, Mrs. Margie Howell, Miss Maggie Belle Hyatt and Miss Carrie Sue Allen. Mr. Jimmie Hyatt accompanied them on the guitar.

Rev .B. T. Turner, pastor for Mt. Zion and Maize Chapel delivered the afternoon message. He took his text from Isaiah 35:2, which reads, "It shall blossom abundantly and rejoice, even with joy singing, the glory of Lebanon shall be given to it, the excellence of Carmel and Sharon. They shall see the glory of the Lord. The Excellency of our God." He expounded on God's Excellency.

Church adjoined and folks waited around for the evening service. The Usher Board of River View Baptist sold homemade ice cream for ten cents a cup.

With the evening session, praise service began at 7:30. Mrs. Ada Howell led the praise service with songs, scripture and prayer. There were congregational songs and even a testimony or two. Now the evening message was about to begin. Rev. J. C. McElrath of Asheville and pastor of the host church took his text from Galatians 1:6, which reads, "I marvel that you are turning away so soon from Him who called you in the grace of Christ to a different gospel." He titled his sermon "Pay Day."

It was said, "Did not our hearts burn!"

Mrs. Katherine L. Wells reported in The Church and Advocate, "The services were well attended and enjoyed by all. . . Collection for the day- $116.05. Usher Board received from ice cream-$10. Grand total $126.05."

That was good day spiritually as well as financially. Splitting the monies equally between Webster Baptist Church, Mt. Zion Circuit, and River View Baptist, each church received about $42.17.

Amen.

This photo of the Feast in the Wilderness is from 1951. l-r: Mrs. Beulah Lackey, Miss Mary Wells, Mrs. Katherine Wells, Mrs. Mellie Chavis, Mrs. Rosie Love and Mrs. Hattie Lackey.

'Fessor Wade: The Man in the Middle
Scotts Creek/Freeze Hill

When Professor John H. Davis retired as the principal of Central Consolidated School, Professor John W. Wade became the principal. For a long time, he was caught in the middle of the Jackson County School and some unhappy black parents. It seemed that these parents wanted Professor Ralph Davis, John Davis' son, to be the next principal. Supt. W. Vernon Cope hired an outsider from Murphy, North Carolina by the way of Bluefield, West Virginia.

He was born on July 26, 1913 to Rev. and Mrs. Frank Wade. His mother, Mrs. Pansy, taught school in the segregated school system in Bluefield. Professor Wade grew up as an only child because his sister died when she was five.

With his mother being a teacher and his father a preacher, Prof. Wade could have chosen either profession. Respectability was important to the black masses and those two occupations ranked high in the black community.

Education was important; therefore, he went to Bluefield State College, an all black school, and obtained a Math and Business degree. While at Bluefield, he was an outstanding football player. He went on to the University of Cincinnati for his Masters.

He met his wife, Mae Louise Sudderth, when he came to Murphy to teach at Texan, the small community of black folks. For the next four years at Texan, he was principal and Supt. Cope personally went to Murphy to persuade him to led Central Consolidated into the twentieth century.

In 1941 while in Bluefield, the young couple gave birth to a son, which they named John William Wade, Jr. Now they had to move to Sylva. Cope assured him that a house would be waiting for him. Just a few feet from the school situated on a little knoll set the principal's home. They moved over the summer of 1942.

While at Central Consolidated School, Prof. Wade became the leader of change, and instituted many improvements. By 1948 all teachers had grade A certificates. The school organized a PTA and affiliated itself with the North Carolina Colored Congress of PTA. Parents were actively involved with their children's education. Now a black child from the county could obtained a high school diploma instead of just going to the tenth grade.

The old plank building was slowly dying. A small smoldering fire had burnt a hole in a fire resistance material in the gym when they fired up the potbelly stove for a basketball game. The school's classrooms' heat came from individual potbelly stoves and plus there was no inside plumbing, which included a water fountain. Modernization had not come to Central Consolidated, but the superintendent assured them that they had the best run school in the county.

Repeatedly going to the board did not help, but a proposal was made that Jackson, Macon and Swain should establish a central high school in Sylva to accommodate all three counties. However, the plan fell through when the Supreme Court decided that blacks were not getting an equal education in their own school.

With the proposal off the table, Prof. Wade and other black leaders still demanded a new school. The new school was finally built in 1956 and the Black students were elated. It was brick with indoor plumbing and central heating. As the next school year came around, Prof. Wade received an offer to become principal at Charles Hall High School at Alcoa, Tennessee. He decided to remain at his post for one more year to see the 1957 class graduate.

While here, the Wade's had three other children, Marquinta, Beverly, and Van Buren. The family joined Liberty Baptist, where, Professor Wade became a deacon, Mrs. Wade played the piano and the two girls sang in the junior choir with director Mrs. Edith Howell.

An early morning fire destroyed the Wade's home, but the love and charity the black and white communities showed was great. The family moved to a house on Freeze Hill. But then, it was time to go and he did. And even after he left, Professor Wade continued to educate himself, earning his Master degree in Administration and Supervision. On January 25, 1960, Professor Wade died while working on his doctorate degrees at New York University.

Aunt Della: The Good Samaritan
Montieth Gap

Aunt Della, as the white folks called her, was born Mary Delaware Casey in February 1879 at the Will Thomas estate in Whittier. She lived there until she was about thirteen years old. Her parents, Mr. and Mrs. William H. Casey brought about 45 acres of mountain tract land from M. L. Deitz and his wife D. J. Deitz for $300 dollars.

While living in Whittier, she believed that slavery still existed. In an interview with The Cullowhee Yodel in the spring of 1930, she told them that her mother was a slave of Kunnel Thomas whose descendants now live in Waynesville. The Yodel quoted Aunt Della, "When my mammy was freed; I was just a chile, and then we moved to Cullowhee." Moving from Whittier to Cullowhee meant freedom to Aunt Della.

With her freedom, Della needed a job to help support her family. She worked as a domestic servant in and around Cullowhee. Sometimes she received Mason jars instead of paper money. If she was paid, it was only about quarter a week. Aunt Della did not mind. She was helping folks out and giving some to her family. Her mother, Amanda could use the Mason jars to preserve food for the winter.

Around the age of 24, she met and married Mr. Edward Alston. Mr. Edward was from Haysville, North Carolina and much older than Della. He was born May 23, 1866 a year after the Civil War ended.

He was a rock mason and searching for a job in the Cullowhee area. The Cullowhee Normal School began to build and expand. Therefore, he got a job with one of the construction companies.

As the twentieth century moved into the 1920's, Ed and Della had six children. The baby Marion was just one-year old. With no work for Ed, they moved to Asheville for a little while. Sometimes, he left

Della and came back. Della was not happy. She wanted the comfort of her home in Cullowhee. She moved back in 1926 and began searching for a job. The only thing she could do was housekeeping and babysitting. Again, she worked for the white folks.

The Cullowhee Normal School was now Western Carolina Teachers College (WCTC). The school's expansion had taken the black Methodist church and graveyard. They built another dormitory beside Moore Dormitory. Therefore, she decided to apply for a job on campus. One of her daily jobs was to work for Professor and Mrs. J. J. Seymour who was a teacher at the college.

In 1928, she obtained a job as a housekeeper at Moore Dorm. She continued to work for Mrs. Seymour after she finished her duties at the dorm. Sometimes Mrs. Seymour lent Aunt Della to other Professor's wives who did not have a regular maid. She was always willing to help anyone who was in need.

Moving from place to place to build rock walls, chimneys and fireplaces, Mr. Ed came home. His failing health prevented him from working, and in June 1935, he became totally unable to work. On May 14, 1939, Mr. Edward Alston passed away.

When World War II began for United States, Aunt Della's baby boy Sherman joined the Army. The Army shipped him overseas to France right in the middle of the war zone. His commanding officer Colonel James Norestien sent Aunt Della a complimentary letter.

The letter expressed that Sherman had proved his valor in facing the enemy on the battlefield in France. Proudly, she showed the letter to Mrs. Seymour, who promptly felt that it was news worthy of local news. Mrs. Seymour took it to The Sylva Herald and they printed it. Aunt Della was very proud of her son.

Aunt Della grew up in the church, whether it was Mt Zion AME Zion Methodist Church or Mt. Carmel Baptist Church. Whichever church had services, she and her family attended.

Aunt Della worked for WCTC from 1928 to 1945, then at the age of 66, Aunt Della went to New York with Professor Seymour and his family. She worked for them for seven more years. She died in 1952 and they shipped her remains home, where she was laid to rest with Ed and her family.

Vester Arnold: World War II Veteran
Arnold Hill/Scotts Creek

At the age of eighty-three, Vester Arnold departed this life, after surviving World War II. He fought in the Pacific campaign as the Japanese attempted to take over all of the Pacific Islands. A lifelong resident of Jackson County, Vester was fondly called Mr. Coon Arnold.

On April 26, 1920 Coon was born to Mr. John Washington Arnold and Mrs. Linnie Love Arnold. As a young boy, he became a member of Liberty Baptist Church where his parents attended.

At the age of thirteen, tragedy struck, when his father died on September 18, 1933. At the time of his death, Mr. John Arnold was only 55 years old.

Mary Ella Mingus was the daughter of Frank and Naomi Whittenburg Mingus. She was born in Dillsboro on September 19, 1922 and joined the River View Baptist Church as a young girl.

Coon and Mary Ella fell in love and married around 1940. From that union a son was born on July 23, 1941. They named him, Robert Orlande Arnold.

Shortly after Japanese attacked Pearl Harbor, Coon enlisted in the United States Army. Like other young men of Jackson County, he went off to fight for his country. After he was honorable discharged, he came home with medals for his conduct and bravery in the Pacific campaign. The medals he received were the American Theater Service Medal, the Asiatic-Pacific Service Medal and the World War II Victory Medal.

On returning home, he found Ella had given birth to another child. She had named him Lewis Franklin Mingus, no father's name was listed on the birth certificate. She had left their home in Sylva and moved in with her mother. The couple tried to patch things up, but it did not work.

Again tragedy befell Coon. It seemed that Lewis had gone hunting and returned home, standing the gun up in the corner. Bobby began to play around with the gun and Lewis told him to leave it alone. With the gun leaning in the corner on its stock, Bobby accidently stepped on the trigger as he attempted to put it back in the corner. The gun went off and the shot hit Bobby in the abdomen.

Bobby was rushed to C. J. Harris Hospital. It was to no avail. Bobby died on that August day in 1952.

Mr. Coon was never the same after the incident. He had lost his only son. Eventually, Ella and Coon divorced. In 1954 with her son, Lewis, Ella left and went up north to Detroit, Michigan.

In the meanwhile, Mr. Coon found a soulmate, Litter Jo Howell. The couple moved in together. By this time, he was employed at Western Carolina University in Cullowhee. He worked in the maintenance department as a maintenance technician.

Although he never remarried, Coon fathered six children. The mother of five of these children was Litter Jo Howell, his soulmate. Their children, which took on their mother's last name, were Phil, Sammy, Ronald, Donald and Janice Howell (Williams).

The mother of the other child (Gretta Worley) was Dorothy Worley. When he retired Mr. Coon spent his time fishing and hunting coon. He liked to play baseball. As he got older, he attended the ball games and watched his children play at the local high school Sylva-Webster.

Liberty Jubilee Singers
Tannery Flats/ Hog Rock/Peter's Bluff

In the late 1940's and the 1950's, a black quartet formed in the county. All the members attended Liberty Baptist Church. However, they came from difficult parts of the black communities. Diversity in the black community and the association with each helped the communities bond. With Thomas A. Dorsey flooding the airways with his songs, it was natural that black folks across the United States would establish their own gospel group. The blacks in Jackson County did just that.

The Liberty Jubilee Singers was a family affair. All but two members were blood relatives, but the other member was a sister-in-law to a member of the group. They were products of the county and their ancestors were slaves. However, some of their families came here from bordering states after the Civil War.

The man who held the group together was Mr. Farrell Dorsey. His father was preacher, Rev. Conley Dorsey. An itinerant minister, Rev. Dorsey belonged to Scotts Creek Liberty Baptist Church. He served many churches in the area and married Miss Candace Love, who was Mr. Farrell's mother. In the church's 100th Anniversary booklet, Rev. C. Dorsey was among nine ministers called Gospel Sons of Liberty Baptist Church. For the closing sermon of the 70th Annual Session of the Waynesville Association, Rev. C. Dorsey preached. At that time, in 1945, he was the pastor of Shiloh Baptist Church in Kingsport, Tennessee.

The Church Advocate in the Sylva News reported the following:
"Rev. Dorsey is one of Sylva's own and we are
proud of him and the progress that he is making
in Kingsport. It was a great treat to have him with us."

143

Being a member of Liberty, Mr. Farrell was very active in church affairs. He was a Deacon and the Sunday School Superintendent. In 1971, he was chairman of the Deacon Board. When a fire destroyed the church, he was on the rebuilding committee. With his wife, he organized a group of young ladies for activities, both spiritual and social. When there were no afternoon services, they went on field trips to Tremont and other places. During basketball season, they played games with other black counties black city teams.

Mr. Farrell's wife, Mrs. Annie Murray Dorsey, was the daughter of Mr. John and Mrs. Lula Murray, who came to Jackson County from Georgia. They came to escape from the place that had held them in bondage. Moving away mean freedom and the Murrays found their freedom in Jackson County in the Scott Creek area.

Mr. and Mrs. Farrell Dorsey had a son, whom they named Farrell Dorsey, Jr. Unfortunately, he drowned in a swimming accident when he was about thirteen years old. The grieving parents continued to work in the church and surround themselves with other children and youth adults.

In the late 1930's Farrell and Annie worked in the Coffee Shop. They were among the cooks in 1939 who work there. Like all colored folks in Jackson County, they worked for the white folks, whether it was at their homes as a domestic servant or in their business as cooks.

Another member of the group was Mrs. Jessie Allen Casey. She was born in Hog Rock to Mrs. Lawrence and Hattie Allen. She went to a one-room school in Webster and met her future husband, Mr. Henry Casey there. When she married, she already had a child, Keldon Eugene (Billy). The couple had children, but they died either at birth or shortly afterward. However, Uncle Henry reared Billy as his own child.

Aunt Jessie belonged to Webster Baptist, but moved her membership to Liberty Baptist. She was a member of the choir and the senior missionary circle. Like Mrs. Annie, she was a member of the Sylva Women's Club.

The other two members of the group were siblings. Margie and Harold Dorsey were Mr. Farrell's cousin from Andrews, North Carolina. According to school records, their mother was Mrs. Christian Dorsey.

Margie Lee was freshman at Central Consolidated when she dropped-out and married Clifford Casey in November of 1947. At one point in her life, she stayed with Mrs. Fredericka Love and helped her.

Harold was also a student at Central Consolidated. He stayed at his cousin, Mr. Farrell's, home. He was an excellent singer and an accomplished guitarist.

After Margie married, sometimes Harold stayed with his sister in Peter's Bluff where she made her home with her husband, Uncle Clifford. It is in Peter's Bluff that Harold and Margie became acquainted with Aunt Jessie, who lived next door. Aunt Margie and Aunt Jessie became friends.

When the idea came about group, it was natural that they would ask Aunt Jessie to join and Miss Maxine Whittenberg, who belonged to Liberty. Her parents were McKinley and Janie Mae Whittenberg. She could sing as well as play the piano. The Liberty Jubilee Singers sang at different church events and accepted out-of-town engagements. Harold played the guitar and was the lead singer. Aunt Margie and Aunt Jessie sang background, while Mr. Farrell was the spokesman for the group.

They sang the latest black gospel songs like Thomas A. Dorsey's *"We'll Understand it By and By," "Precious Lord, take my Hand," "Let Jesus Fix It for you,"* or perhaps *"There Will Be Peace in the Valley."* Whatever gospel songs they represented to their audience, it was well received.

The Liberty Jubilee Singers traveled in Georgia and South Carolina, as well as the Western North Carolina counties. Everywhere

they went, Harold Dorsey sat the tone with *"How I Got Over."* As this song became the group signature song, the audience requested it if it had not been sung as the program ended. Sickness and other events dissolved the group. Aunt Jessie became a victim of tuberculosis and by the time she recovered, the group had split up. Aunt Margie went up north and her brother Harold left the county, also.

Aunt Margie, Miss Annie, Aunt Jessie with Uncle Henry with Cousin Bob on his shoulder.

The Lackey Men
Cullowhee/Gudger Hill

As slavery ended, black folks drifted into the area from the surrounding counties. One of these families was the Lackeys. They moved from Haywood County and settled in Cullowhee area. Mr. William Jeffery Lackey and his wife Mrs. Lela Parrish Lackey and family came around 1914. Some of their children were born in Dillsboro and Webster areas, which meant that they constantly moved. Finally, they bought land from the heirs of Thomas Davis just above Mt. Zion.

Settling in the area and finding jobs, the Lackeys had eleven children. Their children were James William (1988), Daniel Gehove (Hovey), Theodore (1901), Charles O'Nell (1902), Elf Edward (1905), David Wilburn (1909), Samuel (1912), Isabella (1915), Otelia, Robert (1917), and Maudine (1923). Being churchgoing folks, they joined Mt. Zion and worked faithful.

Their oldest son, William and Samuel both died in 1937, but before he died, Will married Carrie Fisher of Webster. They had a daughter, Mildred, who died at the tender age of nineteen.

Robert was born on May 18, 1917. He married Hettie Robinson and had one child, whom they named Robert Lee. He worked as a truck driver for a construction company. When he died in 1986, he was about 80 years old. In the meanwhile, Robert Lee married Annie Bell Studderth and had three children. They were Robert Lee, Jr., Oliva Anne, and Roberta L. In 1953, he was working at the Sylva Hospital as an orderly and living in Webster.

Mr. Theodore Roosevelt Lackey married Hattie Rogers. She was the baby daughter of Mr. George Rogers and Mrs. Josephine Gibbs Rogers. After they got married, they resided at the old homestead with her unmarried brother, Earnel Rogers. Mr. Theo worked at Western Carolina Teachers College as a custodian. He and his wife worked and supported the church. Mr. Theo became the preacher's steward. As the preacher's steward, he handled the money for collection and made sure the preacher got his salary each Sunday. Mr. Theo passed away on November 8, 1978 and Mrs. Hattie laid him to rest in Mount Zion AME Zion Cemetery.

Elf Edward was born March 2, 1905. Like all his siblings, he attended one of black one-room schools in the county. With the automobile becoming the mode of transportation, he became a mechanic. He worked in a garage in Webster. On January 26, 1939, tragedy struck. He was found beaten and rushed to the hospital. However, they could do nothing for him. He was dead on arrival. The law investigated his death, but could not find any suspects. They ruled his death a homicide, but stated on the death certificate that person or persons unknown killed him. It is a cold case that will never be solved. All suspects are dead and possible witnesses have long gone to their graves.

Charles O'Nell married Miss Beulah Lowery. She was the daughter of Mr. William Anthony Lowery and Mrs. Mary Casey Lowery. They had two daughters, Mary Lela and Annie Ruth. Charles lived with his in-laws and worked at Western. Like his brother Theo, he was a custodian. During the 1940's Mr. O'Nell was a welcome sight to many young frightened students who attended WCTC. Being away from home, he had a smile for homesick freshmen. When World War II began, he visited all the young men who were drafted into the military. Not only did he visit them, he hugged and told them that he would be waiting their return.

A man of compassion, Charles gave Ralph Roberson, a student a pair of his overalls when he and Ralph were on cleanup duty. It was cold, Mr. O'Nell had on two pairs of overalls, and Ralph did even have a jacket. Without hesitating, he removed his outer overalls and gave them to him.

Charles' job went beyond being a custodian. His daughters Mrs. Annie Ruth Lackey Lash and Mrs. Mary Lackey Hooper recalled that their father frequently brought home students who were in need of a good homecooked meal. The Lackeys always provided starving students a meal.

By the late 1950's and early 1960's, he worked on the night shift at Breese Gym. When my twin brother was in high school, he and cousin, Robert Lynn would go to work with Mr. O'Nell. They enjoyed it because Mr. O'Nell cleaned up the gym after a basketball game. Victor and Bob met the players and shot basketballs after the game. Additional benefit was to watch a college basketball game.

When a basketball outlived its usage for the college level, Mr.

O'Nell retrieved it from the trash. In turn, he gave the ball to Victor and Bob. Sometimes, the two boys donated the balls to our school. Usually those worn out balls were in better shape than the ones we had.

Mr. O'Nell believed that education was very important. He attended the newly formed PTA in 1948. The PTA appointed him to represent the Cullowhee area on the City Service Committee. Just as all his family, he became a member of Mt. Zion at an early age. He attended services regularly and actively participated in church functions.

After serving both black and white communities, Mr. O'Nell retired from Western that had become a university in 1967. He had seen the school grow, as the black population decreased. More and more people were leaving and that included his children and their family.

Prior to his retirement in 1963, his grandson Johnny Bryson came to live with him. It was time of the Civil Rights Movement. Jackson County had not really been caught up the frenzy. A new school for the blacks had been erected and integration seemed far off.

However, the next year, young parents decided that integration was important to the education of their children. Among them was Mrs. Merlelia, Johnny's mother. When approached about integrating the school system in Jackson County, she agreed.

Mr. O'Nell watched as his grandson became one of the first students to integrate Camp Lab School in Cullowhee. Earlier he witnessed the first black student to enroll at Western. She was not fulltime student, but came to a summer school session.

On July 14, 1973, Mr. O'Nell passed away. He rests in the Mount Zion AME Zion Cemetery, where he can look down and see his church.

In 1991, a group of WCTC alumni of the 1940s officially dedicated a marker to the memory of Mr. O'Nell for the important part of their college lives. On a summer day in August, a headstone placed on his grave read: "Friend to WCTC Students, Loved by All Who Knew Him."

David Wilburn Lackey was the third son of Mr. and Mrs. William Lackey. He was born March 8, 1909 in Haywood County and educated in the segregated school system. Wedding bells rang for David when married Miss Frances E. Love in the late 1920's. Their first child was a boy and they named him David Wilburn Lackey, Jr. David Jr. was born on March 6, 1931 and died the next day.

Their second child was a girl. Doris was born around 1933. She grew up in the segregated school system and attended Central Consolidated School. She went on to Lincoln Academy in Kings Mountains. After she graduated, she attended Winston Salem Teachers College for two years and a semester State Teacher College at Fayetteville. She went to New York.

In the late 1950's she went to Philadelphia and attended the Franklin School of Science and Arts. She received a diploma in X-Ray Technology on June 23, 1960. She did her internship in a hospital in Jamaica, New York After graduation Miss Lackey obtained a job in the New York City Department of Public Health.

The David Lackey's third child was Walter Ray. He was born in 1935. At the age of two, he died. Without a male heir, Mr. Dee, as he was affectionately called, found other boys to teach them to play the guitar. He taught my brother, Medford and William Allen to play. Mr. Will Rogers' grandsons, Tommy, Dennis and Stanley wanted Mr. Dee to teach them to play the guitar. Each boy had his own small instrument. The first time they were there, Mr. Dee told them stories that fascinated them. Therefore, the boys returned with the notion that Mr. Dee would spin another tale. Usually, the guitar lessons were forgotten, as the boys enticed him to embellish another story.

Growing up in the hollow of Peter's Bluff, on any given afternoon, one could hear the melody of the guitar from just over the hill. Everyone knew it was Mr. Dee. He played beautiful music that plucked your soul.

Unlike his brothers, Mr. Dee never learned to drive. He walked everywhere he went. Rarely did he go to church, but his wife, Mrs. Frances and their daughter Doris attended the church, which was just a nice stroll from their home on Gudger Hill. Like Mr. Dee's parents, they belonged to Mt. Zion AME Zion Methodist Church.

Mr. Dee was a construction worker. He helped build homes in the area. On Gudger Hill, he built his home and planted grapes and apple trees on the hill above his home.

It was said that Mr. Dee could embellish a tale of old. With his music, he enriched the people around him. At Harris Regional Hospital on December 6, 1997, Mr. Dee quietly passed. His guitar will forever be silent.

Miss Susie and Mr. Charlie:
Sacrifices for their Children's Future
Long Branch/ Scotts Creek

Miss Susie Bryson was born on August 1, 1908 just over the hill in Buncombe County to Mr. Jack Love and Mrs. Mellie Rogers Love. She came to Jackson County in 1915 and stayed with relatives on Long Branch. At the tender age of seven, she began school in the segregated school system in Jackson County. Living in the Long Branch area, she attended the one-room black school on College Hill.

After schooling, she met and married Mr. Charlie Bryson in 1927. Mr. Charlie was born May 1, 1903 to Mr. John C. Love and Mrs. Estella Coward Love of Jackson County. He received his schooling at the one-room African American school in his district. When Mr. Charlie obtained a job at the Tannery, the couple moved to Sylva. While Mr. Charlie worked at the Tannery, she found day work. She became the day maid for Attie Brown, the owner of The Sylva Ruralite.

For the next eighteen years while she worked for Attie, she had four children. Ruby was born in 1929, Hazel Marie was born on March 6, 1930, Charles Jr. was born on March 16, 1932 and Bobby Curtis was born on April 18, 1934. She and Mr. Charlie wanted all their children to obtain a college education. It would be difficult with $6.60 salary Mr. Charlie received from the Tannery and the measly $1.00 a day she took home from her day maid's job. Their total income for the month was about $46.40. Mr. Charlie Bryson worked for the Tannery for about thirty years. And there was no chance for advancement.

The couple sacrificed for Ruby to attend Allen Home for her 11th and 12th grade years. In 1947, Ruby graduated from Allen Home and enrolled at Winston-Salem Teacher's College. This cost more money. Besides that, Hazel would finish high school that next year. Unlike Ruby, Hazel did not have to go to a boarding school to receive her high school diploma. In 1948 Hazel was among the students who were the first 12th grade graduating class from Central Consolidated School. Monies were needed for both of the girls' college education.

How were they going afford to pay for both girls' college fee? Since Livingstone College was affiliated with the AME Zion Methodist Churches, Hazel got a scholarship from the Salisbury, North Carolina College.

Not too far behind the two daughters were their two sons. Charles Jr. and Bobby C. started their high school career at Central

Consolidated School. However, they took advantage of the opportunity to finish elsewhere to prepare them for college. Charles Jr. went to Lincoln Academy in Kings Mountain and graduated in 1949, and then he enrolled at North Carolina A&T College.

To complete his high school requirements, Bobby went to John Chavis High School in Cherryville. After graduation, he also went to A&T. Bobby graduated from A&T in 1953, while Charles dropped out after his first year. He joined the Air Force.

Miss Susie and Mr. Charlie made many sacrifices for their children's education. It was estimated that price tag for one year of tuition for all four of her children was about $800 dollars.

Where were they going to obtain the funds to put them through college? Both Miss Susie's and Mr. Charlie's job did not pay enough. They needed to seek other employment. Another day maid job was not going to do it and obtaining a raise at the Tannery was out of the question. Therefore in 1944, Mr. Charlie headed north to Detroit, while Miss Susie headed just over the hill to Western Carolina Teacher's College. Both were employed. Mr. Charlie found a job as a carpenter and Mrs. Susie obtained a job as a maid at the Library at WCTC. In the Church Advocate in the Sylva News for November 18, 1944 stated:

"Mr. Charlie Bryson, who has been in Detroit, returned home Saturday, where he will spend the winter with his family."

Mr. Charlie and Miss Susie grounded their faith in God. They belonged to Maize Chapel AME Zion Methodist Church in the Tannery Flats. They held many positions in the church and held the

church together until they departed this life. Miss Susie was member of Missionary Society, a Deaconess, Daughter of the Conference Worker for 20 years, and church secretary for 40 years. She also was acting Superintendent of the Sunday School. Like his wife, Mr. Charlie worked in the church. He served as Superintendent of the Sunday School, Class Leader, Chairman of the Trustee Board and Preacher Steward. He was also a member of Lodge #591, TuckaseigeeValley Prince Hall and the Grand Lodge FSA Mason of North Carolina.

They were proud of their children. Ruby graduated from Winston-Salem College and became a teacher. Hazel graduated from Livingston and went north to work. Charles Jr. made a career in the Air Force, remaining there 21 years. Bobby graduated from A&T and got a job at Ohio University in the lab.

Just Over the Hill

With the onset of the 1950's a new era began in the history of the African Americans in Jackson County. We had our own destiny in our hands. The old ways were rapidly fading. African Americans became part of the majority of the population. We championed causes in our neighborhood to make it a safer place for our children to play. Becoming part of the establishment, a token black became a member of a board or an organization.

When the Supreme Court decided that the white and black schools were not equal, the ground work was laid for us. In 1954, the white school at Cullowhee wanted the Streater boys to play basketball, but integration came too late. It was during this that the African American amateur baseball team disbanded. The migration of the young black men in the county was one of the causes. Another cause was the ballfield was slowly dying.

There were second and third generations of African American teachers, but they did not stay long. Most left and went down the eastern part of the state or they migrated to the North.

Instead of integrating the school system, a new building for the colored students was erected in 1956. It was brick, with central heating. There was a kitchen to serve hot meals for the students. Most important there was inside plumbing and a central heating system. The older African Americans, who no longer had children in school, approved of the plans.

Hence, integrating was postponed until 1965. The year before total integration, young black parents went to board for some action. A select number of African American high school students were allowed to attend the all-white high school in their district.

By that time a new principal at Jackson School had been hired. All was lost. The African American students were short changed, as they continued their studies at Jackson School without any extra curriculum activities. Their only sport was basketball.

Leroy Leonard McDonald: Buffalo Soldier/Janitor

Dillsboro/Tannery Flats/ Scotts Creek

On December 12, 1916, in Macon County, just over the hill from Jackson County, Leroy Leonard was born to Mr. Lester and Bessie Scruggs McDonald. Leroy was the second child of the couple. Two years earlier, their first son, Lester Jr. was born August 3, 1915. Over the years, Lester moved his family to Dillsboro where James Edward was born. In 1931 the first child to be born in Jackson County to Lester and Bessie was a girl and unnamed.

Eventually, the family built a house in the Scotts Creek area where they joined Liberty Baptist Church. An article in the Sylva Herald in 1960 stated that Leroy was born and reared in Sylva, attending the public school Colored Consolidated School, which was the all black school in the county.

It seemed that Leroy serviced his country as well as his community. He joined the United States Army on September 18, 1941 and did his basic training at Fort Bragg, North Carolina. After basic training, he was stationed in Omaha, Nebraska during the winter months. While on guard duty in 1942, he suffered extreme frostbite of both feet. This caused Leroy to limp when he walked; however this did not prevent him from going overseas for his country during World War II. He served more than a year in North Africa with the United States Army in the 9th Cavalry motorized units. He was qualified for the MM 30 Cavalry Rifle and other military weapons.

When he returned from overseas, he was stationed again at Fort Bragg at the Separation Center. While at Fort Bragg, his military occupational specialty was the operation of a light truck (345). On November 3, 1945, Leroy was honorably discharged from the Army; at the time his rank was Private First Class. He was decorated with the American Defense Campaign medal, the American Theater Campaign medal, the Good Conduct Medal and the AR 600-68 Victory Medal.

Before Leroy left, he had been a service station attendant and was a driver for 1526 Engine Dump Truck Company. Lester had married, but divorced. He had lived with his parents and was known by his friends and neighbors as Ham. Upon returning from the Army, Ham came home to his family.

In the latter part of the '50s, one of the main wings of the original C.J. Harris Hospital was partially burnt. At that time the hospital was located on Court Hill overlooking the town of Sylva. For 426 hours, the county was without a hospital. In 1960, Leroy obtained a job with the hospital to do cleanup work as the new building was being finished. The hospital reopened on May 8, 1959. However, plans were already in progress to build a new hospital.

The new building was erected on the hill just over from Leroy's parents' home. Now, he had a job with the cleanup crew. When the building was completed he was hired as a janitor. The newspaper article from the Sylva Herald stated that Leroy was doing an excellent job of keeping the hospital clean and spotless and the floor shining.

Although he was assigned to the first floor, he also helped out on the other floors. Like a true Buffalo soldier, Leroy took his job very serious and with pride.

Leroy died at C. J. Hospital on September 15, 1979. He was still living at home with his parents at the time of his death. He was a man who defended his country from the Nazis and took pride in his janitorial job at the hospital in his hometown.

'Fessor Frank: The Lame Duck Principal
Locust Creek

Professor Frank K. Davis took the principal position of Jackson School for the 1957-1958 school years. He knew when he accepted the position he would be the last sitting principal of the all black school in Jackson County.

Integration kept peeking around the corner. Enrollment continued to drop after Macon County established an all black high school for their black students. However, Professor Frank decided to deal with the problem head on. Everything would go on a usual.

Education was the name of the game. That was Professor Frank's main goal. A good education for the mass of black students who entered the school was important. He knew how important an education was because his mother was one of the first teachers in the area. Mrs. Josephine Moore Davis had set precedence for her children and Professor Frank was fulfilling that dream.

Born in 1913, Frank Davis was destined to be a teacher. He went to Central Consolidated School through the tenth graduate. Then Professor Frank went to a private school to obtain his high school diploma. He attended St. Augustine's College in Raleigh and received his B.S. degree. Later he did his graduate work at A&T College at Greensboro and Bishop Trittle School of Social Work.

When he graduated from St. Augustine's, he could not get a job in the Jackson County School System. Therefore, he put his application in at Macon County. He was hired in the segregated school system in the elementary department.

While teaching there he met his future wife, Miss Virginia Gibson. When they got married, he promised her that he would get a job out of state. When he obtained a job in 1940 in his home county, the years went by without any job change. Meanwhile, the couple had two children, Sybil and Roderick.

As a teacher at Central Consolidated, Professor Frank wore many hats. He drove the bus until he became the principal. With Professor Love, they coached basketball and during the season, the boys' team only lost one game. He taught social studies, science, French, Algebra, and 8th grade Math. At one point, he was elementary homeroom teacher, which housed fifth through eighth graders.

Professor Frank never kept his promise to Mrs. Virginia, but at one point in his life, he wanted to take a job in Norfolk, Virginia. However, he turned it down. He became the lame duck principal with the hope that the job in Norfolk would be waiting for him when integration came to the county.

From 1957 to 1965, Professor Frank headed Jackson School, the new brick building situated on a hill. He did not realize that it would take so long. In his heart, he knew that job in Norfolk would not be waiting. When integration did arrive, the Jackson County System would not let him down. They would find a place for him and other local black teachers.

In 1964, Jackson County School System accepted six black students to two of their high schools. Complete integration was not far behind. During that school year, Professor Frank had the enormous task of getting the black students ready for the transition. The faculty had to make sure that each student passed the CAT at the end of the school.

Therefore, Jackson School spent most of its time on academics. All organized sports were banned, but on Friday afternoon, all the students went outside to play.

When the final commencement program came, Earl Hooper, supervisor of Jackson County School delivered the graduation address. All the awards had been given and diplomas awarded to three graduates, the piano key struck the chord and the Alma Mater was played and sang for the last time. Jackson School closed.

The black students registered in the school in their district. It was no longer Professor Frank's responsibility...it would the responsibility of the principals at the once all white schools.

Professor Frank was not worried, for he was sure he would find a place in the county's school system. After all, he was one of their own. The job did not materialize. Professor Frank was not offered a job in the Jackson County School System. The job in Norfolk was gone.   Now Professor Frank was out on a limb and it was cutoff.

Macon County had recently opened a Job Corp center. Built to education intercity boys and girls, the Lyndon B. Johnson Job Corp Center was the brainchild of President Kennedy. Its main purpose was to give those boys and girls a new start in life by teaching them, not only academics, but a trade.

Professor Frank put in his application for a position there. The center hired him and a new teaching career began. Once more he was able to inspire the youth of the country, as he did at Central Consolidated and Jackson School. Dr. Herman Thomas who teaches at Shaw University said that Professor Frank had inspired him to become an educator.

Davis taught at the Center until his death. Ironically, he began his teaching in Macon County and he ended it there.

Miss Grace: A Safe Place to Play
Tannery Flats

Mrs. Grace Dorsey Bryson was a mother with a maternal concern for the safety of all children who resided in the Tannery Flats. She was Girl Scout leader for the black girls in Jackson County and one time president of Jackson School PTA.

A monument to her affords to keep the children from playing and running the streets of the community is Bryson Park. This park was Mrs. Grace's dream long before integration. The white children had Poteet Park, which had an area for little children play and an outdoor swimming pool with lifeguards.

The safety of the black children at play was her objective. She had seen her nephew Farrell Dorsey and Jimmy Jackson drown because they had to swim in the creek or the river. She spearheaded the project to get a playground for the black children to play safely.

Born on February 1, 1904, Mrs. Grace was the daughter of Mr. Sol Dorsey and Mrs. Minnie McDowell Dorsey in Jackson County. She was educated in one of the black one-room schools in the county. As a young girl, she joined Liberty Baptist Church. As a member, she served loyally. She was president of the Missionary for 19 years and president of the PTA for 16 years.

Her husband, Mr. Odell Bryson was born August 15, 1902. His parents were Mr. John Bryson and Mrs. Janie Babb Bryson, married on May 31, 1920. Like Mrs. Grace, he was born in Jackson County and went to the one-room black school in the Sylva area.

This union resulted in 17 children, with none of them multiple births. Fourteen of their children reached adulthood. Their names are Sol James, David, Doris, John Robert, Odessa, Emma Lou, Richard, Billy Dean, Jane, Minnie Jo, Yvonne, Jacqueline, Linda, and Farrell.

To support his growing family, Mr. Odell operated a laundry, which was attached to his home. He served both black and white customers.

Over the years, Mr. Odell slowly lost his sight, but continued in the laundry business until his health would not permit him to operate. Mrs. Grace did her part to keep food on the table and clothes on their back. She worked as a domestic servant to several white families in the Sylva area.

Having that many children, she involved herself with school activities. When the PTA organized in 1948, she became the vice-president and a Grade Mother for the elementary department. The duty of the grade mothers was to organize parties and other extra curriculum activities. She was also responsible soliciting help from the other mothers in the elementary department. It was the grade mother's job to be sure that the teacher had all the school supplies for the children.

In the early 1950's, Mary Wells was hit by a car on the main road in the Tannery Flats. She was not seriously hurt, but Mrs. Grace became afraid that the next time it could one of her children. Therefore, she decided to do something about it.

The children needed a place to play without having to watch out for cars. She thought the area where the red company houses were located would be a perfect spot for a playground. She solicited the help of Rev. Joe H. Smith who was the pastor of Liberty Baptist Church and some other parents.   Together, they went to the Board meeting of the town commissioners. Rev. Smith was their spokesperson.

Mrs. Grace continued to pursuit the matter. Finally, the town commissioners did something. When Poteet Park was appropriated monies by the commissioners to buy new equipment, the Tannery Flats got the old playground equipment. They cleared the area of debris and leveled any red company houses that were still standing. After, the equipment was put in the park, they built a basketball court with two regular size goals.

Bryson Park is named in honor of Mrs. Grace Bryson, who was a woman of grace. She was quiet, but forceful when it came to welfare of the children.

Mrs. Grace passed away in 1969

knowing that her grandchildren and great grandchildren had a safe place to play from sunrise to sunset.

Uncle Clifford: Farrier and Firefighter
Peter's Bluff

In the past on the Fourth of July, John Parris wrote… "A nostalgic reminder of the pioneer past comes alive…when the nation's oldest wagon train rolls out on 100-mile journey through the mountains…" This was the 24th year of this wagon train and among those taking the trek was Mr. Clifford Casey from Peter's Bluff, a little community of Cullowhee.

It was 1982 and this was Mr. Clifford's fifth trip as the wagon train's farrier. If a mule or horse threwa shoe, he was there to put it back or replace it.

Uncle Clifford was born on May 27, 1921 to Mr. George Casey and Mrs. Sadie Hooper Casey in Montieth Gap community. His father was a blacksmith and operated a shop in Cullowhee. During the 1930s Papa George taught all nine boys the art of blacksmithing, especially the fine art of shoeing horses and mules. However, only Uncle Clifford, Uncle Henry and my dad, Estus took up the trade. Like Uncle Clifford, my dad shoed horses for folks around Jackson County.

Downtown Cullowhee, 1930s

When Papa George shoed horses, the customers usually came to

162

his shop in Cullowhee, and then he continued his trade when he no longer had the shop.

Papa George traveled all over these mountains to shoe horses. In the modern times, the farrier is known as an itinerant shoer, who takes his tools and makes house call. Uncle Clifford had been shoeing horses most of his life. With an inference on mountain heritage, Uncle Clifford became part of the mountain heritage celebration at local schools in the county.

In 1984, he demonstrated his skills at the Spring Folklife Festival at Blue Ridge School in the Cashiers Community, which is just over the hill in Jackson County.

Uncle Clifford obtained his formal education at Central Consolidated School in Sylva. After the attack on Pearl Harbor, he enlisted in the Air Force with his buddy, Abraham Pettit, Jr. When the war ended, he returned home. In November of 1947, he married Miss Margie Dorsey of Andrews, North Carolina. The marriage lasted for a few years. They parted company and obtained a divorce. In the late 1950's, he married Miss Annie Frances Tate of Long Branch in the Cullowhee area.

He built Aunt Frances a home in Peter's Bluff on land he bought from Uncle Charlie Casey. They lived there until he died in Asheville at Memorial Mission on August 14, 1985. Aunt Frances maintained their home until she was unable to provide for herself. Today she resides at Morning Star Assisted Living.

When the Cullowhee Volunteer Fire Department organized through Western Carolina University, Uncle Clifford joined. He was the first black person in Jackson County to join the all-white volunteer fire department. At the time, Uncle Clifford was a janitor at the university and had become the supervisor of the janitorial service.

Uncle Clifford was well respected in both communities. The Cullowhee community honored his hard work and dedication as firefighter after his death. Story as it that he arrived on horseback at the scene of a fire before the fire engine arrived. Indeed that is dedication and devotion to his job. He was employed by WCU for 35 years before he retired in 1983 as a supervisor.

Besides being a member of Cullowhee Volunteer Fire Department, he was on the board of Trustee at C. J. Harris Hospital (Harris Regional).

Church was important to him. He belonged to Scotts Creek Liberty Baptist in Sylva, while Aunt Frances held membership at Mt. Zion AME Zion Methodist Church in Cullowhee. Because of his two marriages, he could not become a deacon, but he served as treasurer of the church. However Uncle Clifford served as the chairman of the Trustee Board, Church Treasurer, and Assistant Sunday School

Teacher, member of the Usher Board and a member of the Layman League.

Although he did not have any children of his own, Uncle Clifford loved to be around them. During the summer, his nephews and nieces from both sides of the family stayed with him. He fed and clothed them. He gave them money to spend. In other words, he showered them with his generosity and his love.

Uncle Clifford favorite saying was. "I be doggone it, I be doggone."

Streater Star Athletics: "Watch the Ceiling Boys"
Cullowhee

The saga of the Streater boys is legend in Jackson County, even before their offspring played and made a name for themselves at Sylva Webster High. Their names were William Harvey, Herbert Dean, and Willis James Streater, Jr.

The older brother Harvey finished the tenth grade at Central Consolidated High School (CHS). Afterward, he and his cousin Bill Burkes went to John Chavis High School in Cherryville, North Carolina to complete their high school education. While at Cherryville, he and Bill participated in the high school athletic program, which included football, basketball and baseball. At that time, CHS did not have eleventh and twelfth grades. It only went to the tenth grade

Other members of the 1949 Central Consolidated High School basketball team went over the hill to complete their high school education. Bobby C. Bryson also went to Cherryville, while Charles Bryson and Richard Powell attended Lincoln Academy in Kings Mountain. Hershel Love graduated from Reynolds High in Canton and Garland Fair moved to Stephens Lee High in Asheville. Major Wells traversed way over the hill to Washington D.C. where he lived with rela-

*1949 CHS Baskeetball Team. (l-r) Garland Fair, Harvey Streater, Major Wells, Bobby C. Bryson, Hershel Love, Charles Bryson & Robert Hampton. Back row: Coach C.L. Love, Bill Burkes, Mack Powell, Richard Bryson * Coach F.K. Davis.*

tives. He attended Dunbar High.

In the meanwhile, Herbert Dean and James remained at CHS. They played basketball and made a name for themselves in the county. Both of them finished their high school career at the school. At the annual banquet in 2000, Jackson County's Athletic Hall of Fame recognized the 1953-1954 basketball team of Central Consolidated School for their accomplishments.

That season they posted a 21-1 record and won the Piedmont Conference. Along with Dan Bryson, Charles Pickens and Charles Norman, they were the starting five. The tournament voted Herbert Dean Streater the Most Valuable Player.

Herbert not only played basketball, but also was an important part of the football team the school put together with the help of the white community. There was no baseball team at school. However, he played baseball with an organized all-black club in Sylva called the Red Sox. His little brother Willis James also was an excellent basketball, baseball and football player. He played running back and tight end on the football team. Small, James could fly. Like his brother, he played for the all-black baseball club.

When James graduated from high school, he continued to play basketball on a black Jackson County city team. The team consisted of former CHS players from Cullowhee and Sylva. They played other black city team. They called themselves the Tigers. Harvey also played with Cullowhee/Sylva Tigers.

In two games of the Tigers were recorded on two homemade score sheets. On January 30, 1957, the Tigers defeated the Waynesville Dribblers 50-25. Both James and Harvey played. Harvey scored 17 points and James netted eight. Without a date, on the other score sheet (playing Franklin) Harvey again scored 17 and James had twenty. The Tigers won 71-42.

Who were these three Streater boys from Cullowhee? Until they learned to drive, the boys took the long bus ride to Sylva to Central Consolidated School. Once learning to drive, the boys bought a car and drove themselves to school. They were the sons of Mr. Willis James Streater, Sr. and Mrs. Ada Rogers Streater.

Mr. Streater came from Chesterfield, South Carolina. He was born December 26, 1891. Coming just over the hill to Western North Carolina, he looked for a job and found love with Miss Ada Rogers, daughter of Mr. George Rogers and Mrs. Josephine Gibbs Rogers.

Settling down, they had one other child besides Harvey, Herbert Dean and James Streater, Jr.

All the Streater children were athletic, which included the oldest child, Miss Margaret Josephine. Miss Margaret became a teacher and taught at Central Consolidated. After she graduated from Fayetteville State College, she obtained her first teaching job in Andrew, North Carolina. While there, she met Mr. Ray Miller and married him.

Returning to her home county, she became the primary teacher at CHS. Mrs. Miller coached the school's girls' basketball team in the late 1950's and 1960's. She remained the girls' basketball until the school closed in 1965.

Playing basketball and football for Central, the all-white school in Cullowhee heard of their skills. In the wake of the 1954 Supreme Court decision about separate, but equal was not equal, integration entered the athletic department of the county's white high schools. The Streater boys would make a welcome addition to their basketball program. The coaches did not see the benefits, but their players did.

However, the all-white schools never got a chance to play with the original Streater boys. Graduation came for the boys who were born in 1930s. Integration came too late for them. Their athletic feats remained buried in history and in the archives of the Sylva Herald. The tiny gym where they played has long since been torn down. Any trophies the school won are buried in a trash dump, but if you lived that life, you remember. Sticking in my mind is the voice of Texana School principal of Murphy, North Carolina. Sitting on the stage which served as the bleachers for the basketball game, she shouted to her players, "Watch the ceiling, boys! Watch the ceiling, boys!"

Indeed, Harvey, Herbert Dean and James watched the ceiling. It was not high enough for them, but their sons were able to shine on in the athletic field. Their accolades were confined to the trophy case of the black school, but their sons' athleticisms drew the attention of all Western North Carolina and beyond.

James Streater's sons, Jimmy, Stevie and Eric were inductees in the Jackson County Athletic Hall of Fame. They displayed their athletic skills in football, track, and baseball at Sylva Webster High. Herbert Dean's son Herbert returned home to play football on the collegiate level at Western Carolina University.

Again, let us repeat the Murphy's principal's words, "Watch the ceiling, boys!" The sky is the limit.

First Tooth Pulled at 82: Miss Rose Ann
Tannery Flats/Cullowhee

On Wednesday, September 19, 1984, Mrs. Rose Ann Dorsey had her first tooth pulled. She was 82 years old. All her other pearly whites were still in excellent shape in her mouth. In her lifetime, she had never had a tooth filled.

At the time, Mrs. Dorsey was living in Cullowhee at the Center for Assistant Living. Being in the center, it was difficult for her to obtain the things she needed to maintain her healthy teeth.

Born on May 10, 1902, in this mountainous region, her family practiced the old fashion ways to keep her teeth healthy. Instead of a store bought toothbrush, her family used black gum to clean their teeth.

Her parents were Mr. Adam Bryson and Mrs. Odelia Bryson. According to her death certificate, her given name was Janie Roseann. Through the years, her first name was forgotten and she became Rose Ann.

She was educated in the segregated school system of Jackson County at the one-room church school beside the Liberty Baptist Church, where she obtained a 7th grade education.

When she was about 13 years old, she met Mr. Henry Dorsey who was about 39 years old. Shortly afterward, they married. No one knows whether it was an arranged union by her parents or if Rose Ann had been swept off her feet. At any rate, on November 24, 1917, the couple had a child, Annie T. Dorsey. In 1926, another child was stillborn. A year later, Ruby Janie Sue was born on March 31, 1927 and their last child, Mary Ellen was on March 6, 1930.

Mr. Henry Dorsey was the son of Mr. Sol Dorsey and Mrs. Harriet Wilson Dorsey. The Dorsey's came to this mountainous region from just over the hill in Tennessee. Mr. Sol met Harriet in Jackson

County and married her. The couple belonged to Liberty Baptist Church and their children joined when they were young, which included Henry, who was born on January 7, 1878.

Being young, but marrying an older man, Mrs. Rose Ann continued the old ways of doing things. Money was hard to come by. Mr. Henry was a common laborer, which meant he did odd jobs for the white folks in Sylva. Mrs. Rose Ann kept house and raised their daughters.

From her parents, she had learned to clean her teeth with black gum tree twigs. Although modern times had produced manufactured toothbrushes, Mrs. Rose Ann felt that a black gum toothbrush and the use of snuff attributed to her good healthy teeth. Many times, she sent her children out into the woods to obtain some twigs of black gum to clean her teeth.

When Mr. Henry died on July 5, 1939, she found herself alone with three children to nurture. Annie was grown, while Ruby was twelve and Mary Ellen was nine. Now Mrs. Rose Ann had to join the work force. She went into the food service. She worked in the hotels in Sylva and eventually obtained a job at WCTC in Cullowhee. Upon retirement, she worked in the kitchen of Jackson School, the modern segregated school for Black children. She worked there for nine years, until Jackson County finally integrated the school system.

Upon retirement for a while, Mrs. Rose Ann Dorsey lived with her daughter Ruby in Waynesville. However, she loved to fish. She came back to Jackson and sat on the banks of the Tuckaseegee. Silently, she sat chewing on black gum twig or dipping snuff. Whiling away the time, she waited for the fish to nibble her bait so she could reel it in.

Time passed and Mrs. Rose Ann needed to have someone to take care of her. Ruby was busy trying to make a living as a cosmologist. A decision had to be made. Mrs. Rose Ann loved Jackson County where she was born. Therefore, Ruby found an assistant living home in Cullowhee. Now, Mrs. Rose Ann could not find black gum twigs to clean her teeth. She had the modern toothbrush to slide around her gums and teeth. Her snuff was not taken away, but without the black gum twigs to clean her teeth, decay sat in. Hence, on that fall day of September 19, 1984, Mrs. Rose Ann Dorsey had her first tooth pulled.

Mrs. Rose Ann Dorsey died on August 21, 1990, at the age of 88.

Miss Frederick:
Her Children Followed in Her Footsteps
Tannery Flats/Scotts Creek

On October 7, 1899 land was purchased for the first African American school. It was one half acre of land located on the bank of Scott Creeks in the vicinity of the present day Scotts Creek Liberty Baptist Church.

Within a year, the African American community in the Beta/Scotts Creek area built a one room frame building. Therefore the school became a social center with the newly freed African American. Already, they had freed themselves from the white Scotts Creek Baptist, which was organized in a log cabin in Beta. With erection of the school, the church family moved to worship in the tiny one room school.

The Trustees of the newly formed Scotts Creek Liberty Baptist Church purchased one half acre of land on December 8, 1903, which adjoined the school property. This would be the site of the church. Within three years, the church was completed.

By 1910, the church organized under the leadership of Rev. Richie. The first Deacon Board and the first Missionary Society were established. From these organizations emerged a leader of the church who continued to influence the church members into the 1970's. Mrs. Frederick Matilda Wilson Love became the secretary of the Missionary Society and her husband Mr. Clarence Lorenza Love became a member of the Deacon Board.

Born in Sylva on March 1, 1881, Mr. Love was the son of Mr. Richard Love and Mrs. Ellen Bryson Love. He was a common laborer until he obtained a job at the Tannery at the turn of century. At the Tannery, he became a beamer.

On the other hand, Miss Frederick was born around 1890 in Buncombe County, which was just over the hill. She was perhaps education in the segregated school system of Buncombe County and went to a normal school to earn her teaching certification. She came to Sylva to accept the job as the teacher of the little one room school on the bank of Scotts Creek and became a permanent resident when she met Mr. Love and became his bride.

The couple perhaps met at one of the social gatherings at the church. At any rate, they were married around 1910. On May 14, 1911, the couple had their first child, Marjorie Moletha. Six years later they had another child Clarence Love, Jr. He was born October 19, 1917.

When the public school took over the church school, Mrs. Frederick M. Love retired to raise her children. Being a former teacher elevated her position. That meant she could read and write. In 1971 she was still the secretary of Senior Missionary Society.

With her education, it gave her status in the black community. Traditionally, it is told that Mrs. Frederick was a staunch Baptist and discouraged any church member from attended the black Methodist Church that sat right in the middle of Tannery Flats. When Liberty did not have services on the second and fourth Sundays, she advised them not go to Maize Chapel.

Ironically, although the Loves lived two doors down from Maize Chapel, she never went. After Sunday school, when there was not going to be any services at Liberty, most of the members would go home. On their way, they had to pass the Methodist church.

Her children, Marjorie and Clarence went to the segregation school system in the county. By the time they finished their education the black school had consolidated to Sylva. Like their mother, both of them became school teachers and taught at Central Consolidated School.

Marjorie became an elementary teacher and taught at that department for a few years. She married A. R. Wilson and moved to Hackensack, New Jersey where she continued to be a teacher. Moving north was important for the couple because of jobs opportunities for her husband. The tannery closed and the Mead Corp. moved in and they did not hire African Americans to work on the assembly line.

Clarence Jr. became a science teacher after being educated at one of the all black college just over the hill. He returned home and began teaching at Central as the high school science teacher. While at Central, he started a football program, which lasted for two seasons. It became difficult to have enough students to fill a team.

Eventually, Clarence followed his sister and headed north. His destination was Columbus, Ohio. He applied for a job at Ohio State University and was hired as a professor. His wife Lillie Mae Davis was a school teacher in the Clay County segregated school system in a one room school in Andrews. Being a teacher, it was easy for her to obtain a job in the public school system in Ohio.

Mr. Clarence and Fredrick were very proud of their children. They were professional and successful individuals. Most of all they had followed in their mother's footsteps and became teachers.

Their father, Mr. Love died in 1950 at the age of 69. Mrs. Fredrick lived until the 1980's. Although she persuaded a lot of the members of Liberty Baptist Church not to attend the black Methodist churches in the county, her children did.

Mrs. Fredrick Matilda Wilson Love was a teacher, a staunched Baptist, a wife, mother, and a midwife. She influenced many people in the African American community in the Sylva area.

Casey Brothers Managed Black Baseball Teams
Cullowhee/Sylva

In the 1950's and 1960's baseball once again became the favorite sports for the African Americans in Jackson County. Their home field was the baseball diamond at Central Consolidated School on the bank of Scotts Creek. During that time three different Casey brothers managed the team or teams. They were all sons of George Power Casey and Sadie Hooper Casey.

These Black baseball clubs played on most Fourth of July. If they played in Sylva, the bleachers were full. Hotdogs, sodas, and popcorn were sold at these events. It was not only the local African Americans who attended the games, but the stands were integrated with white fans, who rooted for the home team. It was an annual event that helped celebrate Independence Day.

Both Cullowhee and Sylva had a team. Often, they played each other as the colored fans from both sections of the county came out to cheer the home boys. Cullowhee's was called the Cullowhee Slow Sluggers and the Sylva team was called the Red Sox. These two teams would play each a lot. It became a friendly rivalry.

At that time Henry Casey managed the Slow Sluggers. Topnotch players like Billy Casey, Bill Bennett, Robert Lee Lackey, David Bennett, Herbert Streater and Andrew Hampton graced the field. Some folks said that at that time, Andrew was best catcher in the county. In 1955, Cullowhee ended the season with a 15-5 record.

There were many thrilling games as the African American teams slugged it out; however, the most thrilling game between Cullowhee and Sylva was in 1956. With score was tied at the end of regulation play, the fans remained seated as the game went into extra innings. The tenth inning went by...the eleventh inning went by. Being the boys of the summer, darkness held out until nine o'clock or so.

At any rate, by the end of the twelfth inning, the game was still tied. Sylva managed to retire Cullowhee in order. It was the bottom of thirteenth inning and Sylva needed only that one run to win. With two out and a runner on third, Jesse Howell lined a hit up the middle and Sylva won.

Although Cullowhee lost, many of the Sylva players joined the

Slow Sluggers. It seemed that outward migration was depleting both teams. Therefore, they came to the conclusion to combine the team and keep the name Sylva Red Sox.

Shortly afterward, Henry decided to retire and let some of the younger guys manage the team. In his days as a manager, the Cullowhee Slow Sluggers traveled to Tennessee, Georgia, and South Carolina to play other African American amateur baseball teams. For Henry, it was time to hang up his cap.

Sylvester Love took the job with Clifford Casey helping him. By 1958, Clifford managed the team by himself. With Clifford in charge, the club had a winning season. They rolled over just about all opponents.

Two years later Lyndon Casey became manager. With the caliber of pitchers like Bobby Allen, Harry Howell and Jesse Howell, Jr., the Red Sox went undefeated. At the end of the season, the boys of summer had racked up a 13-0 record. Riding high on their 1960 accomplishments, their opponents came after them with all their best. By midseason, the Red Sox had experienced their worst season ever. Sylvester returned and helped Lyndon to look to future and forget the terrible season.

With Bill Casey's retirement from the game, they were in need of a catcher. The club found a few rookies eager to play with the veterans. Among those rookies was 6 foot, 170 pounder Joe Love, Sylvester's son. He tried out for the position of catcher and won it with his accurate throw to second and the ability to effectively to block the plate.

Another rookie, Bob Mebane, the Casey boys' nephew, won the shortstop position with his quick hand to throw from his position to first. Bob also was an excellent pitcher. His specialist was his curve that had the batters shaking their heads. Joe's older brother William was a great outfielder and like Bob, he could pitch. Herbert Conley, whose grandfather Wilse Dorsey who was a great player, was a good relief pitcher. Later the team used him in as a starter.

With those fine rookies, it appeared that the Red Sox was going to win lots of games. They had veterans like Dan Bryson, Charles Jackson, Harvey Streater, Charles Pickens and playing manager Lyndon Casey.

Besides the rookies and the veterans, the team hoped to renovate the ball field and fix more seating capacity for the fans. However, the opportunity to do it never arrived. Jackson County could not hold the young African Americans here. Migration took them away. With the manpower gone, the all black club disappeared. The boys of the summer were gone just as the ballfield slowly crumbled with neglect.

The Casey boys hung up their gloves. Years later Lyndon Casey appeared on the scene when Little League was integrated.

Again, Lyndon was coaching, but this time it was the 11 and 12 year old Little Leaguers. Henry and Clifford had other things to do. Therefore, they hung up their gloves forever. All three joined in the family fun to play softball at family reunions.

From Jook Joint to Church House:
Supt. C. W. Johnson, Jr.
Tannery Flats

In the late 1950's the African American church organization of Church of God in Christ (COGIC) made its present known in the African American community of Tannery Flats. Unlike the Methodist and Baptist churches, it was established by African Americans after the Civil War. In 1886 Charles H, Mason and Charles Jones from the Church of God organized the church, after being dissatisfied with the methods of teaching and the presentation of the Bible message. They took their message to streets and any pulpit that would allow them to speak. The first structure that Mason and Jones could find was a jook joint in Mississippi. Even the building COGIC rented in the Tannery Flats would be similar.

By the mid 1960's the Church of God in Christ had made its way to the little mountain county of Jackson in Western North Carolina. Wesley Quives of Washington D. C. came to Jackson County with the express pursuit to open a holiness church which would be connected to the Asheville District of COGIC established in 1939.

Mr. Wesley Quives was married to Katherine Rogers, a local girl. Together, they came to Jackson give the African Americans a new religious experience. From the Asheville District, Superintendent C. W. Johnson, Sr. sent his son Elder C. W. Johnson, Jr. as the pastor for the church. This was Elder Johnson's first charge.

Finding a building to house the church wasn't too difficult. Mr. Jim Wells, who was a deacon and a member of the River View Baptist Church, owned a two-story block building in the Tannery Flats. At this time in history, the lower part of the structure was not in use. In the beginning, the lower unit was a restaurant, which served the African American community. It was considered a jook joint because it had a jukebox to entertain the customers. There was a dance floor where the patrons could jitterbug until the joint closed. Besides the eating and dancing, they gambled their hard earned money on a Saturday night in and around the building.

The location was perfect for it was situated in the middle of the largest African American community. And this new Christian holiness religion could obtain some converts. COGIC was different from the Baptist and Methodist churches. Although both the Baptist and Methodist believed in the Holy Spirit, it was never really explained to their members. In the Methodist Apostle Creed, it states..." I believe in the Holy Ghost, the Holy catholic church..." Although members faithfully recited this creed, they never questioned it.

In COGIC, they explained the Holy Spirit and other religion statements from the Bible. According to the Bible, the Holy Spirit is the comforter that Jesus left to protect us. In other words, their belief was that God was the Son and the Holy Spirit all roll into one. In other words, it was the Trinity. Although the Baptist and Methodist believed in the Trinity, it was just lip service. For the members of COGIC, it was more than lip service. The Holy Spirit engulfed their body to make them shout, dance and holler. It grabbed them, and they sometimes talked in tongues.

Deacon Wesley Quives took care of the church while Elder Johnson traveled back and forth from Asheville. During the week, Deacon Quives drove the African American school bus. That was excellent job, because the African American school, Jackson School, was about a half mile up the road. That meant that he could park the bus in the parking area at the school and then walk down to the Tannery Flats to see about the church.

At the time of the establishment of this COGIC church, the AME Zion Methodist Church and Liberty Baptist Church conducted services on alternating Sunday. The Baptist church had a full church services on the first and third Sundays and Maize Chapel (Methodist) convened on the second and fourth Sundays. On the fifth Sundays, all the churches had services together, which were called the Feast in the Wilderness. By this time, Liberty had withdrawn from the Feast in the Wildness and organized its own Fifth Sunday Meeting with other African American Baptist churches in the area.

It seemed that COGIC had no intention to rob the established churches of their membership. Therefore, it was decided they would meet in the afternoon when either the Baptist or the Methodist conducted service. As a result, some of the members of the Methodist church and the Baptist church worshipped with them.

Rev. Richard Bryson, son of Mrs. Grace Bryson and his family became a member of the church. Others in the African American community became affiliated with COGIC.

When integration of the school occurred, COGIC closed its doors. The established members moved back to Washington D. C. because of lack of income. Rev. Bryson and his family headed to South Carolina.

Like the first COGIC church in the Tannery Flats, the Methodist Church closed its door because of the lack of membership. Being a family church, the family members migrated to the North and the older members died.

When Mrs. Susie Love Bryson died in December 1990 and her daughter Rubye Fleming returned north shortly afterward, Maize Chapel closed its doors when the next Annual Conference came. There were only about three members left. They were Mr. Alvin Conley, Mrs. Barbara Blakely Rogers, Ms. Victoria McDonald, and her infant daughter, Faustine. The pastor was Rev. Mary L. Jones, who was assigned to another church. With the defunct of Maize Chapel, the small congregation joined Mt. Zion in Cullowhee, or other dominations.

The church stood empty for almost seven years, when Bishop Adam West bought it. Today, God's Holy Tabernacle, an independent Church of God in Christ, occupies the structure in the Tannery Flats that once was Maize Chapel. Bishop Adam West and his wife Rev. Cyritha Rogers West co-pastor the church. The door opened again in 1998 and was dedicated to God. On September 12, 2010 Bishop Adam West and his first lady Rev. Cyritha West will celebrate their 12th anniversary. The building is once more a sanctuary of God, just as the land was purchased for that purpose 97 years ago. The rented building where the first COGIC church was located was torn down by the county in 2008.

Avon Calling: Miss Mildred

Tannery Flats/ Scotts Creek

Avon is ranked first in sales nationwide, with Avon ladies ringing doorbells from coast to coast. The company (California Perfume Company) was founded in 1886 by David McConnell, a young door-to-door salesman from upstate New York.

Mrs. P. F. E. Albee, a widow from Winchester, New Hampshire was the first woman to go door-to-door to sell a popular Little Dot Perfume Set for the company. Other women were recruited and the company became Avon, the hometown of McConnell.

Today, despite the scores of expensive brand names of cosmetics from America and foreign countries, Avon is still growing strong.

In the 1964, Mrs. Mildred Conley became an Avon lady in Jackson County. She was the first black woman in the area to rang the doorbell and announce, "Avon calling."

However, by that time, most Avon ladies did not go door to door. Usually, they left their catalogue at their work places and put it in a designated area where her fellow workers could flip through the catalogue. If they found anything they wanted, they would jot it down on the order form and pay for the articles when the merchandise came.

Mildred worked at Western Carolina University in the housekeeping department. Working from nine to five, she cleaned one of floors of the ladies dormitories. Four or five other ladies were employed there. Most were African Americans who lived in and around her neighborhood. Some of her customers were white. It did not matter. She would place her Avon catalogue in the break room. This insured that all the employees would see it and buy something from it. Even the residents in the dorm could place an order from the Avon Lady.

Besides being a housekeeper and an Avon Lady, Mildred was a licensed beautician. Her shop was connected to her home, which operated on Saturday. Therefore, she could get more Avon customers as she straightened and curled hair for a night on the town or Sunday morning worship service. Some of her customers came just over the hill from Swain and Haywood counties

This money from this and Avon supplemented her income. Mildred had two daughters and a son, and she wanted to help them after they finished high school and embarked on their college career. She understood the value of a college education. In her youth, she attended the segregated school system in Jackson County. Central Consolidated School gave her a firm foundation. Her parents were able to allow her to attend Allen High in Asheville to complete her schooling.

After obtaining her diploma, she began her college career. Regrettably, she had to terminate her college career. At the age of eighteen, she became pregnant. On November 20, 1938, she delivered a son, Conley Stovall Dorsey. That was just eight days before her 19th birthday. According to the birth certificate, the child's father was Robert McDaniel of Macon County, who was nineteen.

Later on, she married Alvin Conley and had three other children. They were Margaret Ann, Herbert Marshall, and Glorinda. Alvin wanted to make Conley his son. Therefore on September 12, 1942, Conley Stovall Dorsey became Robert Taylor Conley.

Mildred Dorsey Conley was the daughter of Mr. Wilson Dorsey and Mrs. Gladdis Enloe Dorsey. She was born November 28, 1919. She was a lifelong member of Liberty Baptist Church, which she joined at an early age and a former member of the Women's Sewing Club. She was also the chairman of kitchen committee at the church.

When she retired from WCU, she volunteered for 10 years at Harris Regional Hospital and the Hospital Auxiliary Store.

Her husband, George Alvin Conley was the son of Mr. Walter and Mrs. Nora McDowell Conley. He was born on January 31, 1921 in Sylva. Like his wife, he attended Central Consolidated School, but he was a member of Maize Chapel, AME Zion Methodist Church in the Tannery Flats, which he joined at an early age and was active in the rebuilding of his church. He enlisted in the US Army and fought in World War II. After he returned home, like Mildred, he obtained a job at Western Carolina University. He worked in the food service at Western until his retirement. However, he went back to work in Western's Housing Department until his death on August 26, 1996.

In the meanwhile, Mildred's Avon business continued to grow until poor health made her give up it up. With congestive heart failure, she was placed in Mountain Trace Nursing Center in Webster. On January 19, 2001 Mildred Dorsey Conley passed away.

Called to Preach the Gospel: Miss Mary
Webster/Freeze Hill

Reverend Mrs. Mary Walton was one of the first African American female ministers in Jackson County. She was born on February 24, 1922 to Mrs. Elizabeth Bradley and David Moore. On her birth certificate her mother, 15 years old, is listed as Lizzie Casey. Husband Mr. David Moore is thirty-three years old. He was not a native of North Carolina; he came to this mountainous region from Florida.

Miss Mary attended the segregated school system in Sylva at Central Consolidated School. As a young girl, she joined the Webster Baptist Church and later moved her membership to Liberty Baptist in Sylva. While at Liberty Baptist, she sang in the choir and her husband, Mr. Charles Nathaniel Walton, played the piano.

In the September 1944 edition of The Church and Southland Advocate, Mrs. Elizabeth Gibson announced the marriage of her daughter, Mary Moore to Charles Nathaniel Walton of Asheville. Mrs. K. O. Wells reported in the Dillsboro News that the wedding took place in Clayton, Georgia on August 12, 1944. The couple made their first home just over the hill in Asheville, before returning home to Jackson County.

Mr. Charles Walton was from Buncombe County. He was born on October 6, 1914 to Mr. Albert and Mrs. Bertha Pettie Walton. Mr. Walton was educated in the segregated school system in the county.

He worked as day laborer. He became the janitor when African Americans new school, Jackson School was built in 1956.

After coming home to Sylva, Rev. Walton worked forty-four years for Mr. Sol Schulman, a businessman who owned a clothing store in downtown Sylva. She was employed in his household to clean and take care of the children. Mr. and Mrs. Sol Schulman loved her humble ways and loyalty to their family. Therefore in essence, she became a part of his family

She was a good and faithful church worker, but she felt that God had called her to preach. She enrolled in W. V. Grant Correspondent Bible College in the late 1960's. It was a twelve months course which gave her the title Exhorter-Minister. Being a Baptist, she could not pastor a church, for at that time women preachers were not welcome in the pulpit, and especially consider pastoring a church. However, this did not deter Rev. Walton. She left Liberty Baptist and joined the AME Zion Methodist.

Before she left, she earned two certificates from the Southern Baptist Seminary Extension. These classes were also correspondent courses. Determined to become a minister, Rev. Walton earned a diploma from the Faith Clinic Crusade. Through this course, she learned the workings of a church, which included finances, strong relationship, marriage, time-management, family enrichment and other situations a pastor must be able to handle.

With these credentials under her arm, Rev. Walton joined the ranks of other women pastors/evangelists in the Blue Ridge Conference of the African Methodist Episcopal Church. She became the assistant pastor at Mt. Zion AME Zion Church in Cullowhee where her close friend and colleague Rev. Mrs. Maria Hayward began her ministry. While at Mt. Zion, she was elected President of the Missionary Society, Assistant Chairperson of the Stewart Board and a member of the Deaconess Board.

With scarcity of male ministers in the Blue Ridge Conference, Rev. Walton was able to secure a ministerial post in small rural churches in the conference. Those churches were old traditional Methodist churches, which had slowly lost their membership through death of the older members and the migration of the majority of their young African Americans. Most male preachers did not want to be burdened with the financial responsibilities of small churches. Most of these sanctuaries were circuit churches. It would take the patience of a woman to find ways to raise money for the assessments, the conference assessed them.

Rev. Walton took on the challenge. Each Sunday morning, she drove to her charge and ministered to her people. She was the shepherd and they were the sheep.

Before Reverend Mrs. Walton stepped down from the pulpit, she pastored four small churches.

She not only pastored in Western North Carolina, she journeyed to Tennessee and Georgia. As Methodism goes, it can assigns a pastor for four or so churches, continually moving her between churches. On any given Sunday, she spent about eight hours to and from her home and back. When she traveled to Shaw Creek in Horseshoe, North Carolina, her hours doubled.

When Mr. Walton was not at Liberty playing the piano for the Senior Choir, he went with her. If no one was available, their adopted daughter June Theresa Howard would accompany her mother.

A tall, quiet man, Mr. Walton's artistic ability as a pianist was recognized by the church, Liberty Baptist, when they had an appreciation celebration.

Rev. Mrs. Walton and Mr. Walton complimented each other. Rev. Mrs. Walton always had smile on her face. She was very social person and could hold a conversation with anyone.

On the other hand Mr. Walton was man with few words. He seemed to think about what he had to say before he spoke. The beautiful music, which came from the piano when he tickled the ivory, spoke for him.

On May 27, 1994, Rev. Walton's husband passed away. When he died, he was employed by C. J. Harris Hospital in the kitchen.

Reverend Mary Aster Moore Walton followed in other women's footsteps, but she was one of the first African American women pastors in Jackson County. Although she had tremendous responsibilities in pastoring multiple churches at the same time, she was indispensable to her family and gave to them with all her heart.